My dearest sister Ellie,

What's In My Heart?
Volume II

More Blessings to you my sister. Take care and God Bless.
Love you,
Sis Esther

What's In My Heart?

Volume II

A COLLECTION OF
INSPIRATIONAL POEMS AND
POETRY SPOKEN
FROM THE AUTHOR'S HEART

Esther B. Jimenez

Copyright © 2011 by Esther B. Jimenez.

ISBN: Softcover   978-1-4653-3671-2
        Ebook   978-1-4653-3672-9

All rights reserved. No part of this book may be reproduced or transmitted in any form or by any means, electronic or mechanical, including photocopying, recording, or by any information storage and retrieval system, without permission in writing from the copyright owner.

This book was printed in the United States of America.

Interior Images and Cover Design By Esther B. Jimenez

To order additional copies of this book, contact:
Xlibris Corporation
1-888-795-4274
www.Xlibris.com
Orders@Xlibris.com
101198

CONTENTS

DEDICATION 15
PREFACE..17
ACKNOWLEDGEMENTS 19
INTRODUCTION..21
FOREWORD..23
ABOUT THE AUTHOR..25

CHAPTER I   INSPIRATIONAL INSIGHTS

    God's Call 31
    What Matters Most?..33
    Remember Me 34
    The Angel 35
    Self-Discipline...36
    Evangelization 37
    Detachment 38
    Blaming 39
    The Divinity 40
    The Lighthouse...41
    The Holy Spirit 42
    Chastity...43
    Dreams..44
    The Road To Happiness 45
    The Road To Success 45
    Struggle...46
    Judge Not..47
    The Silent Thief 48
    The Portrait...49
    The Star Of My Life...50
    Holiness 51

The Pathway To Holiness	52
After God's Own Heart	52
Living In Poverty	53
Spiritual Journey	54
Spiritual Reality	55
Spiritual Hospitality	56
Spiritual Connection	57
In Darkness	58
If... Is One Powerful Word	59
The Saints	61
The Centurion Creed	62
Fear	63
Walk The Talk	64
Lifetime	66
Decision	67
Toast To The Memories	68
Numbers	69
God Is Enough	71
The Now	72
The Moment Of Truth	73
The First Gift	75
Recipe For Love	76
Recipe For Generosity	77
Recipe For Humility	78
Recipe For Kindness	79
Kindness... It Is	80
Set The Captives Free	81
The Dance Of Life	83
One On One	83
A Day To Remember	84
Over-Comer	85
Be Yourself	86
The Gift Of Life	87
Peace	88
Embrace Your Hurt, Embrace Jesus	89
Denial	90
The Last Of The Lasts	91
The Last Judgement	92
A Reason To Live	93

Slow But Sure	93
A Beautiful Heart	94
Reflection Upon Reflection	95
Leadership	97
Blowing Horn	98
Monday! Monday! Monday!	99
Before And After	100
A Bookmark	101
I Believe	102
Virtues	103
Thank You	104
The Real World	106
Will You Take Time?	107
Being A Human	108
Visual Sanctuary	109
Reaction Formation	110
What Shoes Are You Wearing?	111
Pretentious Death	112
Focus On The Good Things	113
Oblivion	115
Generosity	116
Getting To Know You	117
The Bliss	118
The Language Of The Heart	119
Soliloquy	120
Birth Vs. Death	122
Never Doubt	123
The Heart	124
The Book Of Life	125
Great Moments	126
Remembering You	127
A Time To Heal	128
Moments Of Awareness	129
My Struggling Heart	130
Footprints In My Heart	131
Retreat Of Silence	132
The Longest Telegram	133
The Amazing Book	135
Transformation	137

CHAPTER II A POEM FOR EVERYONE AND ABOUT SOMEONE

A Poem For Everyone 143
Our Lady 144
Our Mother, The Blessed 146
To Our Blessed Mother, I Cry 147
Our Father—The Pope 148
Mother Angelica 149
Blessed Are The Handicaps 150
Golden Moments 151
Senior Moments 152
Love At First Sight 153
A Message Of The Unborn 154
Toddlers—Tots 155
Thank You America 156
The Farmer And The Fields 157
The Reformed 158
The Jurors 159
The Mailmen 160
The Firemen 161
The Secretaries 162
The Crafters 163
Special People (In Reading Poetry) 164
A Smile 165
The Retirees 166
The HousekeEping 167
The Carpenters 168
A Teacher 169
Caregiver 170
The Doctor 171
A Nurse 172
That's Her Josie 173
The Clown 174
To Ponder On 911 176
The Punch Line 177
Shortening The Life 178
The Poetry Of The Confused Sheep 179
Prayer For The Good Shepherd 181
The Class '70 Reunion 182

The Fellowship	183
A Confession Prayer.	*184*
You're So Near And Yet So Far	185
A Memorable Weekend	186
The Handmaids Of The Lord	187
Handmaids Of The Lord . . . Cheers	188
Kathy And Sifty	189
My Niece, A Debutante	190
The Eighteenth	191
Chikoy	192
Chini	194
What Must I Do?	196
To My Sister Linda	197
Our Family Treasures	198
The Shared Moments	200
A Grandfather	201
A Grandmother	202
A Father's Vow	203
The Father I Know	204
Father	205
A Mother	205
A Mother's Heart	206
A Son	208
A Daughter	208
My Sister, My Friend	209
A Brother Forever	209
Kisso	210
The "Purr"-Fect Friends	211
Beejay	212
The Crocodile	213
Extinction	214
Perry	215
Memories To Ponder (In Memory Of Perry)	216
Good-Bye Our Perry	218
Lombardo, My Betafish	219
Cookie	220
My Pet "Pong"	221
That's Me Pong	222
"Benjie"	223

CHAPTER III   POEMS FOR THE SEASON

Christmas Is Not X-Mas 229
Christmas Is . . . Love 230
Beyond Christmas 231
It's Christmas Once Again 232
The Ballad Of The Shepherds 234
The Christmas Cards 235
The Spirit Of Christmas 236
Exchange Of Gifts 237
Good, Better, Best 238
Advent 239
Prepare The Way, We Must 240
Seasons In My Heart 241
The Christmas Within Us 242
Four Seasons 244
Begin The New Year 246
The Newness In Us 247
New Beginning 248
The Parish Mission Nights 249
Soup And Salad 250
Forty Days Of Lent 251
The Designer's Mark 252
Were You There? 253
Easter 255
Easter Spring 255
Easter Forever 256
Halloween 257
The Hallow That Wins 258

CHAPTER IV   PARABLES OF THE FABLES

The Parable Of Wisdom 263
The Parable Of Patience 263
The Parable Of Humility 264
The Parable Of Innocence 265
The Parable Of Nature (The Message Of A Blind Boy) 266
The Parable Of Victory 267
The Parable Of Persistence (The Endless Story) 268

The Parable Of Hope 270
The Parable Of Obedience 271
The Parable Of Prayer 272
The Parable Of Gratitude 273
The Parable Of Commitment 273
The Parable Of Justice 274
The Parable Of Wonders 275
The Parable Of Abundance 276
The Parable Of Faith 277
The Parable Of GenerosIty 278
The Parable Of Truth 279
The Parable Of Forgiveness 280
The Parable Of Grief 281
The Parable Of Simplicity 282
The Parable Of Discipline 282
The Parable Of Leadership 283
The Parable Of Suffering 284
The Parable Of Laughter 285
The Parable Of Common Sense 286
The Parable Of Industriousness 287
The Parable Of Self-Control 288
The Parable Of Kindness 289
The Parable Of Courage 290

CHAPTER V   FRIENDSHIP

The Precious Gift, The Friendship 295
What It Means To Be A True Friend? 296
In Friendship 297
A Friend 298
"You" 299
Promises From A Friend 300
The Book Of Friendship 301
Friendly Advice 302
Friendship . . . It Is 303
The Friendship Prayer 303
The Indifference 304
Are You Looking For A Friend? 305
Laughter . . . A Friend Should Possess 305

A Best Friend 306
A Surprise Call 307
I Honor You, My Friend Ching..................................308
My Precious Friend Ching..310
Treasured Moments 311
My Friend, One Of A Kind...312
I Wish I Could 314
My Message To You, In Your Grave 316
To Forgive Is . . . To Let Go.......................................318
For You My Beloved Friend 319
Be An Advocate..320
Subtlety..321
Release 322
Reflection Of Courage 323
In Time Of Need..324
What's In A Friendship? 324
Elizabeth P. Criste . . . Who Is She ?.........................325
Another Best Friend 326
The 80th Birthday Celebration Of Tatay Bert.......................327

CHAPTER VI   ACRONYMS AND HOMONYMS

Definition Of Abortion 331
How To Prevent Abortion 331
Angels, Ask, Bible, Behold...332
Christian, Christmas, Children 333
Divine, Death, Depression 334
Eternal, Eagles, Elephants..335
Father, Faith, Faith, Friends 336
Fishing, Forgive (Prayer)..337
Growth, Grief, Guidance,..338
Holy Spirit, Hope, Hope..339
Heal, Insights, Jesus..340
Jesus, Jesus, Joseph, Kindness 341
King, Life, Life, Love, Love 342
Lamp, Lord's Prayer, Miracles.....................................343
Mother, Mercy, Moses 344
Nurses, Nurses, Obedience..345

Prayers, Prayers, Praise...346
Peace, Perfect, Pals...347
Queen, Rainbow, The Same Man, Savior (Who Is Jesus?) 348
Success, Success, Thanksgiving Day...349
Trusts, Temple, Unity...350
America, Veterans, Veteran's Day...351
Vow, Wings, My X's Prayer...352
Yoke, Zeal 353
The Gift Of Mortification...354

HOMONYMS: Bill, The Trunk, A Bear..355
The Bar, The Tip...356
The Well, Drive...357
The Bit..358

CHAPTER VII THE ABC'S

Beatitudes . . . (The A B C Of The "Be Attitude").................363
The A B C Of Motherhood...364
The A B C Of Personal Growth 365
The A B C Of The Holy Spirit...366
The Alphabet Christian Wisdom..367
The A B C Of Catholic Christian..368
Acclamation! (The A B C Of Worship) 369
The A B C For Hospice Volunteers 370
The A B C For The New Year..371
The A B C Of . . . How To Pray...372
The Alphabet Of Esther 377

DIVERSITY OF POEMS AND POETRY

The Walking Market..383
The Agony Of Waiting..385
Songs' Titles 386
Millennium Song 387
Playback...388
The Allegory Of The Human Body..389
Celebration Of Life . . . Haiku 390

DEDICATION

To my brothers:
Ernie, Rafael and his wife
Lydia, Robert and his wife
Lourna, Rey and his wife
Arleen, and my sister Linda
and her husband Carling,
to Beth, (like a sister to us),
and Rick (like a brother to us).

To my nephews and nieces:
Jay and his wife Evelyn, Rona
and her husband Toffer, Ralph
and his wife Berlin, Jan Carlo,
Joyce, Paul, Chini and Francis.

To my grandchildren and the
future ones:
Christian Jay, Elaiza Jelyn and
Jacob Kristoffer.

This book I also dedicate to my
late parents, Pedro T. Jimenez
and Honorata B. Jimenez.

PREFACE

As I am working with this, "What's In My Heart?" Volume II, the first volume has already been out.

The original plan for the book is to publish just one set of "What's In My Heart?" but I didn't want the book to look like a thick anthology that is heavy to carry. I wanted a handy book that can be put in a lady's pocketbook or at a guy's briefcase or portfolio.

It's easy for me to just write the echo preface from the part one, and I thought of just picking-up some definitions of a poem. But before I do that, let me just explain why I decided to have two Volumes of What's In My Heart?

As I write this preface, I have about four hundred eighty poems/poetry and still writing. I have started writing poems since the year 2000. I have been procrastinating to have them published, until few months ago, one of my close friends encouraged me to pursue the book for publication, and to dedicate it to my parents who passed away few months ago. Then I received a Christmas card from another friend last year, with a short note telling me to start my 2011 with my written poem/poetry be published.

So I have Volume I and Volume II Of "What's In My Heart?" The Volume I has seven chapters: Inspirational Messages; Prayers; Reflections; Conversation with GOD; Nature/Mother Earth; Lamentations; and Self-Expression. The Volume II has seven chapters, too: Inspirational Insights; A Poem For Everyone and About Someone; Poems For The Season; The Parables of the Fables; Friendship; Acronyms and Homonyms; The ABC and with extra chapter (The Diversity of Poems and Poetry.

I have at least twenty-two definitions/descriptions of a Poem in Volume I and I have selected seven of them for my Volume II, the ones that stand out for me.

A poem is a great gift from GOD
A poem is a reflection from the Bible
A poem is found in the Bible pages, (in the Book of Proverbs and Psalms
    of David
A poem for me, aids in the inner healing
A poem for me, is a prayer, a communion with the Almighty
A poem for me, is led by the Holy Spirit
And to be a Poet is one of His gifts.
A poem is like an abstract painting and the viewers are entitled to
their own opinions.

The latter sections composing "What's In my Heart?" present acronyms of diverse words and ideas, which unfold alphabetically, and a separate chapter with just the ABC's (learning the simple and basic rules in life.)

The cover design and all the illustrations in both books are my own paintings/artworks of landscape/nature sceneries. What's In My Heart? Volume I is already out in the market and on lines. What's In My Heart? Volume II is going to be out very soon. Again, what's in my heart is what I would like you to know. Knowing my heart is knowing me. Both volumes are products of my simple creativity and creative simplicity.

ACKNOWLEDGEMENTS

Since this is volume II of What's In My Heart?, I am going to utilize the acknowledgements from the volume I. This is one book with same theme, same number of chapters, same author and just divided into two parts for reading convenience.

I want to thank my beloved parents, Honorata B. Jimenez and Pedro T. Jimenez (who passed away almost a year apart, November 19, 2009-October 26,2010 respectively,) for their utmost love and care.

To my sister, brothers, nephews, nieces, in-laws and cousin Beth for their never-ending support, my sincere thanks to my friends and relatives who patronize my poems, listening to my recitation and giving feedbacks to every poem I write and read, (to you Elizabeth and Monalisa.)

To Barbara Adrianopoli for giving her precious moments to share her reflection on What's In My Heart? Volume I.

To Dr. Geronimo and his wife Gibby, for they are avid fans of inspirational poems, their heartfelt feedbacks to my spiritual and inspirational poems/poetry, thanks to the family.

To Dr Marc Alan Brunelle for his generous time, reading my poems/poetry, of my Volume II of What's In my Heart?, and giving his input and his strong recommendation to read a glimpse of the book.

To my special friend Ching B. Lazo who believed in my ability to pursue my dreams. She is now in heaven fellowshipping with my parents.

Not to forget, I thank the people I encounter everyday, for they act as my reality linear in life. Observing GOD's creations makes me write something about them.

My utmost gratitude to our Almighty for the beauty of nature, His amazing creations and other living creatures (co-occupants on earth.)

I thank You my LORD JESUS, for giving me spiritual inspiration and spiritual direction. For my constant Companion, the Holy Spirit, I am most grateful for the inspiration and His prompts to write this vast numbers of poems.

I can't help but cry sometimes, of how the Holy Spirit prompts me to write such inspirational and heartfelt words from my soul being. Again, I humbly offer my sincere gratitude to the Holy Triune allowing me to feel their Presence.

My devotion and inspiration to our Blessed Mother Virgin Mary, who helps me all the time in interceding for me and with me and for that, I am most gracious and humbled.

My endless acknowledgement t o everyone who revolves in my life and made me realize their importance and to everything that moves my whole being to pay more attention of its essence.

INTRODUCTION

WHAT'S IN MY HEART?, Volume II is a continuation of the first volume. It says about my observations in my surroundings, the focus of my attention. It tells about my messages to my loved ones and friends. It describes the essence of life, (GOD's creations and creatures.)

It offers a collection of verse addressing the types of challenges a person might confront while navigating a path through a sometimes-confusing modern society.

In my heart, I speak of my poems as my daily companion. The Holy Spirit is always prompting me to express my thoughts and feelings, and my appreciation of the beauty of nature through writing.

In Volume II, I acknowledge in my heart the people of different professions. I have acrostic poems, different ABC's in life, and I have shared quite a few parables of my own, utilizing animals as the characters that assimilate fables.

Most of all, my heart speaks loud for GOD's love and mercy, for my utmost gratitude and appreciation, of His Kindness, Goodness and Greatness.

Writing inspirational poems and poetry is one of my great accomplishments. I am given the chance to reach the readers in all aspects of life and indeed has helped me in my healing process, from the grief of losing my parents. The desire of my soul is to invite you to join me in this journey of exploring the reality beyond grasp, that is, the mystery of GOD's power in our lives.

FOREWORD

One thing certain, Esther B. Jimenez's accomplishments in her Inspirational Poems and Poetry take us on a journey to a closer encounter with the Almighty. Her messages are wrapped up in one, with GOD's Call, the Evangelization among them are indeed inspirations that are truly coming from the deepest part of her heart. Her writings become bedtime stories to read to our families. Our grandchildren listen to me read the parables and fables very attentively and make their nights a happy one before going to bed. Esther, as known by her friends, is a very compassionate person. Her love for her pets makes her more admirable for being able to understand the nature of these creatures. As a caregiver of pets, I perceived her compassion towards her pets long before she had expressed "what's in her heart" and it is beyond compare. I thank her and the LORD for giving me the opportunity to listen to the silent messages she is sending through her wonderful works on a journey to the paths of the Almighty.

Robert C. Geronimo, DVM

Robert Geronimo, is a doctor of Veterinary Medicine, a graduate from the University of the Philippines. He is a member of American Veterinary Medical Association and the Venerable Knight Veterinarians (of the University of the Philippines) He is an accomplished private practitioner in Chicago. He worked as a farm veterinarian in the Bureau of Animal Industry and as a Veterinarian for the Pure Foods Corporation in the Philippines before coming to the United States of America.

He met his wife, Gibby Solamillo, an RN, BSN from the Silliman University in the Philippines. Since then the couple established a family with a son, daughter and son-in-law. At present the couple has three grandchildren ages 1, 3 and 7, which are the joy in their hearts.

ABOUT THE AUTHOR

Estrella "aka" Esther B. Jimenez, is a native of Manila, Philippines, a nurse by profession, a US Citizen and residing in Illinois.

Esther is a member of (CRHP) CHRIST Renews His Parish Church, (A Parochial Spiritual Renewal Process), at St. Marcelline Catholic Church, Schaumburg, Illinois. She had offered spiritual talks on the topics of Holiness, Prayer and Scripture, Christianity, Transformation and the Receiving of the Holy Spirit in the Christian community.

Esther is a columnist of Via Times, a Newsmagazine catered to Asian-American community in Chicago, Illinois.

She is also a member of AMG (Authors Marketing Group) of Illinois.

"What's In My Heart?" Volume II, is her fourth published book. The first book is "365 Days Food For Thoughts," and the second is the Bible Tidbits and the third one is What's In my Heart? Volume I. She is one of the authors/contributors of the famous books, "Cup of Comfort Devotional," with two short articles for August 3rd and August 16th daily devotion.

She is working on the following:

    (1) Daily Graces (Prayers Before Meals)
    (2) 202 Turtle Haiku (The Story of Pong-one smart painted turtle)
    (3) Have Phun With Elefants (Elephant Jokes, Riddles, and Knock-knocks with Illustrations), for kids.

She received the Editor's Choice Award in August 2004 and January 2008 presented by the International Library of Poetry. In June 2002, she also was nominated as the Poet of the Year by the International Society of Poets.

In her leisure time, she paints scenery, (landscape/nature), plays the guitar, writes, reads and she goes fishing for holistic therapy.

She loves pet and animals as evidenced by having adorable, beautiful, orange-bellied turtles. One of them named Pong was trained by Esther to dance and to walk with her. Pong likes to communicate with people and he is not aloof, compared to other turtles. Esther is a member of Chicago Turtle Club.

Whatever Esther does, she prays for the guidance of the Holy Spirit and always relies on His power. And for her, the Holy Spirit is her Spiritual Director.

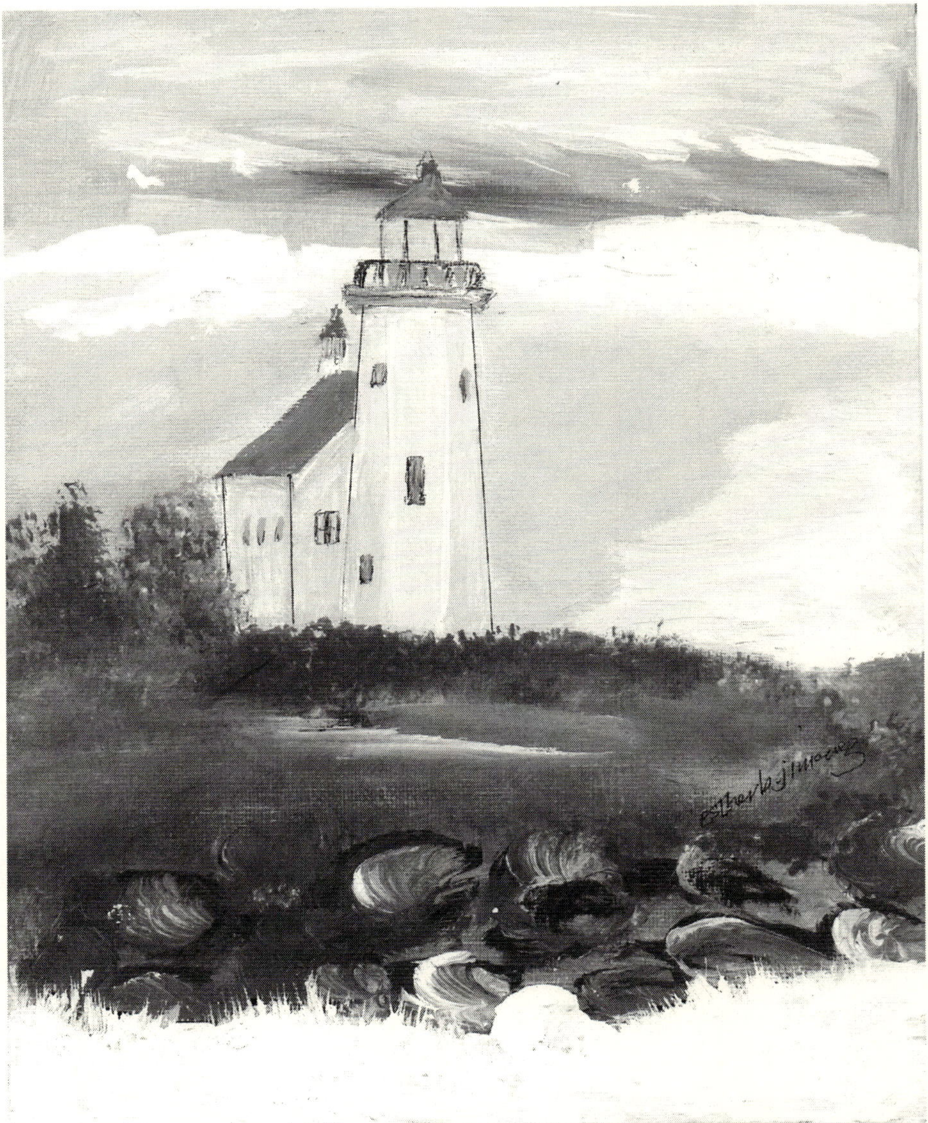

CHAPTER I

INSPIRATIONAL INSIGHTS

In volume I of "What's In My Heart?", there is a chapter about inspirational messages. In this world we need inspirations to drive us to do better, to reach our goals with satisfaction, to do the right thing and to be what we are with ourselves. This chapter will give us insights to inspire us to be whomever we want to be, like the Holy Spirit inspiring me. Let's inspire each other through the Holy Spirit's generosity. Are we in, in the Inspirational Insights? It's time for us to reflect, time for us to have realization of how insightful our lives can be, and time for us to have awareness of the natural and supernatural occurrences in this mysterious world.

GOD's CALL

Knock, knock, knock, who is there, may I ask?
It is GOD, Your Neighbor, knocking at your door
Yes, it is true, our LORD is our neighbor and
He is everywhere
Waiting for us and calling us by name.

You might be a housewife, or might be a truck driver
You might hold a position in a company or you might
be a self-employed
You might be earning a minimum wage or you might
be in six figure income
You might be called, regardless of these reasons.

You might be serving in the hospital, or you might
be solving crimes
You might be defending the accused, or you might
be the guilty one
You are too busy, engrossed with a lot of things
You don't know there is a call waiting for you.

You might be a pre-school kid, or a teenager
You might be an adolescent or a senior citizen
You might have a different color, or you might
be a man or a woman
No one is exempted in the line of GOD's plan.

If you feel the brisk tap on your back
And suddenly you turned your head
then, you looked around and saw no one
that is how it is, when GOD wants your attention.

It's about time to halt for a while from a routine task
To check your messages from GOD
You might be needed to serve in the church
You might be just a good listener to your child.

GOD is the Best Telephone Operator
He listens attentively to those countless calls
He is providing you a Holy line connected to His Son
So start calling Him and start answering His call.

Knock, knock, knock, is no joke game
So open your door and welcome Him
He will fulfill the promise of His love and mercy,
He will connect you to a lifeline, the Holy Trinity.

As for me, I thank GOD many, many times
For calling me at this stage of my life
It's never too late, I always say now
So don't ignore this very important call
"The GOD's Call"

Rring!, Rring!, Rring!
Hello my child, this is GOD calling!
Are You There?

WHAT MATTERS MOST?

In this world we may ask,
"What matters most?"
Is it the clothes we wear?
Is it the food we eat?
Is it how much money we have?
Or the way we behave?

In the workplace, what matters most?
Is it the position we are in?
Is it the six figure income?
Is it the upcoming promotion?
Or the relationship with one another?

In the family circle, what matters most?
Is it the father authority?
Is it the motherhood martyrdom?
Is it the sibling rivalry?
Or the harmonious relationship?

What matters most is how we treat people
What matters most is how we live our lives
What matters most is how we say things
What matters most is, to have the peace in
our hearts.

We are blessed people of GOD
We are indeed created in GOD's Image
We have our Blessed Mother to intercede
We have our LORD JESUS who redeemed our sins
We have the holy angels who sing for us
We have the holy saints whom we invoked
We have the Holy Spirit at our side.
How amazing this life is . . . and that's
what matters most.
How about you . . . what matters in your life most?

Miranda, the five year old girl was talking to a Shih-Tzu dog named, "Benjie," when she uttered that amazing phrase. Let's pay attention to our children's phrases and ponder on them in your heart. Our LORD JESUS loves all children in a special way. Now I know why? We can learn a great deal from them.

REMEMBER ME . . .

"Remember me in your life of destiny,"
uttered by a five year old girl.
Did she know the meaning of that
beautiful phrase?
Did someone tell her about it?
Did she hear it from somebody's lips?
It didn't matter because it's an inspirational
phrase of wisdom.

Remember me when I am at school
learning the basics in life.
Remember me when I start going out with
somebody special;
Remember me when I finish my long
awaited degree.
Remember me, O Almighty whatever I do freely
In this chaotic world it's nice
        to be remembered
        to be noticed
        to be recognized
        to be acknowledged
That there is Someone somewhere
watching us and is always there
to guide our destiny.

Our Sovereign One never fails to be
a part of us, part of our soul and being,
So remember the phrase uttered by a
five year old named, "Miranda",
"Remember me in your life of destiny."

THE ANGEL

You almost fall, you changed your gear
You heard a whisper, that's your angel
Stories told, many times, experiences
With angels, the heroic deeds
The angels heed, each has one indeed.
Watch your back, look around
No one is there, you're safe;
Your protective shield is there
A guardian, very loyal
Angel's ways, mysterious
Angel on my shoulder
Angel with magic touch
Angel on earth
Angel, the Messenger
Angel in disguise
Angel, thank you.
My angel?
Your Angel?
Our angels?
GOD's Angels!

SELF-DISCIPLINE

We learn the word, "discipline" at young age
We are surrounded with laws and decrees
We are bombarded with the word, "don't,"
We are expected to have self-discipline
We are fenced with a lot of temptation
We are guarded by people in uniform,
We are stubborn as a mule,
Let's have self-discipline as a rule.
We are conscious with our body physique
We are indulged with variety of foods;
We ignored the word, "diet,"
We must have self-discipline.
Self-discipline is one of the great virtues,
It applies to everyone and in everyday life
You can discipline yourself step by step
The awaiting reward is indeed great.
If we can discipline ourselves to the fullest
We'll have a better outlook in life
Because we have self-discipline in our hearts
So start disciplining yourself by any means
And ask GOD's grace for this gift
You will indeed have a brighter future
And that includes facing our Creator;
GOD wants us to have a self-discipline
A discipline of having set a prayer time
And that is the best discipline of all
With GOD's grace everything is possible.

EVANGELIZATION

My life is a gift that I should treasure
What I do with my life, is the reflection
of my future
I thank the Almighty for my transformation
The turn point of my life, is my evangelization.
I walked with the steps of the LORD
I learned to be detached from the world,
I gradually changed my life's outlook,
Through the constant reading of the Holy Book
I proclaimed GOD's Good News,
from my heart, thoughts and acts,
I listened to His messages profoundly,
And I started sharing His Holy deeds for me
Thank You my LORD for the real
essence of evangelization
and through the Holy Spirit's guidance
I do now have a deep relationship with Your Son
and that my LORD is the best of
my evangelization
LORD, please continue to grant me the
grace to imitate Your Son, JESUS.
All this I pray in JESUS name, Amen!

DETACHMENT

Vanity of vanities you are so tempting
You give us pleasure and you're so soothing
We're engrossed with material things and
enjoy our lives
But we almost forgot they are just materials.

We buy this, and we buy that, we treasure
the luxury, we dwell on the wealth
We spend lavishly, and throw a bunch of waste
Let's make a change and go for detachment
We'll gain more not in wealth but in health.

Not only in materials are we so attached
Even in relationship and situation as well
We need the grace from GOD to live in norm
The norm to be humble and spend no more.

Detachment is difficult to do
But if we ask GOD's grace we'll be able to
So start listing your attachments
And convert them to detachment.

We can start to have a simple life
And be satisfied with what we have
Just think of the unfortunate people
Who lives on one meal a day and no home at all.

One thing sure is guaranteed here on earth
Is we won't be able to carry anything upstairs
The upstairs I meant is the heavenly kingdom
That is waiting for us, our spiritual advancement.

O LORD our GOD continue to guide us
In our spiritual struggle with our detachment
We want to be attached with You alone
Thank You for our spiritual conversion.

BLAMING

How many times you blamed someone?
How many times you were blamed in your life?
How many times you escaped the truth?
And blaming is the only way that comes forth.
Blaming is a defense mechanism
Blaming eases one's reasoning;
Blaming leads to a habit forming
Blaming can also be stopped
to start a better living.
One thing we should know about blaming
is, it originated from the first beings
Adam (the first man) blamed
Eve (the first woman,) she blamed the
serpent, they blamed each other of their sins
Blaming is very accessible,
Accountability is feasible
But if we start using discipline
blaming will then be in oblivion.
So let's start to be responsible people
from now on, and let's stop the blaming
Let's ask GOD's grace for everything
including the right defense mechanism
Remember, the truth must be revealed
because in truth, we will be freed.

THE DIVINITY

Human flesh, human mind, human ways,
Components and characters of human beings
We think, we act and we behave
We do control everything according to our will.

We feel powerful for we can freely decide
We think they are all our ideas
We plan, we implement and we are proud of our wits
We tend to brag about our accomplishments.

We feel successful, we have accomplished our goals
We celebrate, we rejoice the rewards we received
We spend our time glorifying ourselves
And we forget the Mighty One and His Existence.

GOD, our Almighty, created us in their Image
We humans have limitations but our GOD is perfect
His divinity should be imitated like CHRIST JESUS
And we still can be humans and can do divine ways.

If we think, act, talk and behave divinely
Peace, contentment, humility will be experienced
We can celebrate, rejoice, feel the power of success
In GOD's Presence and all He is, is our guaranty
from here to eternity.
LORD, grant us the grace of holiness and divinity, Amen!

THE LIGHTHOUSE

I view the distance sight
I hear the thunder's sound
I see the lightning streaks
I am your humble lighthouse
I sway along the waves
I dance with the wind
I am here at stormy weather
I am your humble lighthouse.
I am proud to be your guide
I am honored to be your servant
I am glad to be useful
Yes, I am your humble lighthouse.
A lighthouse is a guiding light
A lighthouse is there as a mark
A lighthouse is a symbol of
JESUS, our LORD in our hearts.
So from now on, think of the
Lighthouse when you are
stranded at the water surface,
Always ponder on the Presence
of our LORD JESUS at any given
moment.

THE HOLY SPIRIT

The power of the Holy Spirit started in the
beginning of creation;
Adam was molded from a clay and air was
blown to his nostrils
The existence of life is already there with the
aid of the Holy Spirit
That is the start of the mystery of the Triune.
The Holy Trinity were there at the beginning
GOD said in the Bible, "I will create you in
Our Image", so the "our" is not Himself alone
but, "Two" more of His companions;
it is our GOD, His Son JESUS CHRIST, and
His Advocate, the Holy Spirit.
The mystery of the Triune is unexplainable
GOD is expecting us to trust, believe, and have
faith in Him through His wonderful deeds.
In the New Testament, there are more
empowerment of the Holy Spirit and they are in
The Book of Acts, and letters to St. Paul
The gifts of the Holy Spirit were given to the
Apostles in the Upper Room
These gifts are indeed very powerful tools
Just imagine to have the gift of wisdom, the gift
of knowledge, the power to heal and the power
of discernment, the faith you have, the strange
language you utter, the interpretation of the tongue
were there to receive.
So, let us start to look forward to change our lives
with GOD's grace and JESUS CHRIST's embrace
Let us open our hearts, minds and hands
to receive the gifts already within us,
the gifts of the Holy Spirit.

CHASTITY

Pure heart, pure thoughts
Deeds in purity
Chastity!
Self-sacrifice
Mortification
Offerings
Indulgence
Celibacy
Holy steps to chastity
Great virtue indeed
To chastise in every
Angle of life
Chastity is feasible to do
But without GOD's grace
It'll be difficult
To follow through
Be fervent with your
Prayers
For chastity is there
To obtain
Chastity . . . a holy intention
For purification
A pathway to salvation
Chastity! Chastity! Chastity!

DREAMS

Dreams are mysterious
In our minds, they're subconscious
Dreams are not real, but surreal
Dreams can make you sad and happy
Dreams can make you laugh
Some dreams are weird and funny
Dreams sometimes are answers to problems
Dreams are goals to reach and meet
Dreams are just imaginations
They sometimes stir up emotions;
Dreams are common topics for discussion
Dreams are fun to do wild interpretation
Dreams are inspirations that you look up
for tomorrow
and can be instruments to overcome sorrow
Dreams are only dreams
But dreams are significant in the Bible
Messages are relayed through dreams
to the prophets, the prominent people
One of the twelve tribes, Joseph, son of Jacob
was an interpreter of dreams and because of this,
he became the right hand of Pharaoh.
The angels appeared for few times in the
New Testament, to Mary, Joseph and to some,
Dreams are visions and prophecies in the
Old Testament, and they were fulfilled in the
New Testament.
Dreams are means to communicate and GOD,
Always sent angels to do that
So we should know that dreams are GOD's
Mysterious ways to convey His messages
And so, be positive with your dreams from now on
Don't forget to pray before you go to sleep,
Have a nice dream!

THE ROAD TO HAPPINESS

The road to happiness is paved with the
harmonious relationship, between spouses,
between family members, between friends
and acquaintances, and between ourselves.
Happiness is measured not in richness and
treasure, but in the precious moments each
person spent with the loved ones.
Happiness is giving, sharing and loving;
Happiness is a gift and a true blessing
and happiness is the outcome of the real
peace within.

THE ROAD TO SUCCESS

The road to success is paved with the effort
you have exerted
But first, you must have goals and objectives
then start focusing on your plans step by step
and handle the obstacles positively and its depth;
Being successful is not only in sales
it also pertains to personal relationship
It's about bonding within the family circle
It's how you handle your personal being
To succeed or not to succeed,
there is a road to pave.

STRUGGLE

What does it mean to struggle?
Is it to cope with one's expectation?
Is it the difficulty to reach one's goal?
Or is it a challenge to a success?
Struggle is just like saving oneself
from the verge of drowning;
It is like catching one's breath?
It is like competing to win one's fate
It is like choosing between major things.
Struggle can be physical, mental, emotional
and spiritual;
It is a battle to aim to be better.
But, how will you handle a struggling self?
Just pray, meditate and ask GOD's grace
before you do anything in this world.
Struggle is a blessing that GOD allows,
So in him you can lean.

JUDGE NOT

There is an adage that says,
"Don't judge a book by its cover"
and most of us are guilty of
this saying.
We do say something to someone
facts not knowing
We can't trust our own instincts
in delicate matters
Judging somebody is just like
condemning someone without
a fair trial
Saying something negative without
facts-finding
is a serious case of gossiping
and gossiping is indeed a wrong-doing
So let's stop judging as the Scripture says,
"For as you judge, so will you be judged",
"And the measure with which you measure,
will be measured out to you."
And another thing to remember about judging is
noticing the splinter of others.
Let us remove that splinter from our eyes
and we will see clearer and it will be
reflected on us;
So from now on, let us be non-judgmental
Instead, let's take care of one's welfare,
Let's be sincere in our dealings and show
our Christian ways
Again judge not, so you won't be judged.

THE SILENT THIEF

In the middle of the night it comes to you
You're not aware the silent thief is there
You are in a party enjoying your time
You suddenly collapse, the silent thief reacts.
You are in the hospital as a patient
You're only for check-up; Guess who is there?
          "The Silent Thief ".
You're above 80 years old
You are a newly born
You're at the height of your success
The Silent Thief makes the selection.
Maybe by now you know what
I am talking about
It's the mysterious death known in ages
Death may come upon us like a thief
In the night and launch us into eternal present.
We can't beat death and there is no antidote
But we can have a brighter outlook
That is, we should always be prepared
Like the way, we prepare for the second
Coming of the LORD JESUS.
The Silent Thief, we shouldn't be scared
Just trust everything to GOD even our death.
He will help us to prepare by any means
Including being friend with the silent thief
So let's have peace in our hearts and minds
About the thief roaming around
"Be prepared," as in the boys scouts' creed
Please LORD, just be with us every step
of the way and any moment.

THE PORTRAIT

Image in black and white
Image in different colors
Image printed and developed
That is the portrait of selves.
Photo album filled-up
Collection of memories filed
Films negative to visible positive
The portrait is portrayed.
Pictures can mean a thousand words
People manifest different behaviors
The portrait of life is a miracle
The portrait is a reflection of oneself
In the stillness of the portrait
You can only ponder
And you can use your imagination
To keep the film rolling in your active brain
The portrait of everyone is
The image we carry on
So remember to imitate JESUS
In every move we make
That's the Image we must model
For we are all created in GOD's Image.

THE STAR OF MY LIFE

GOD created us in His Image
We know this fact in ages
He is everything to us
He is the light of our lives
For me He is a Star, that
shines in my dark moments.
He is a Star, that
illumines my mind in a cloudy
time, in moments of resentment.
He is a Star that twinkles,
telling me that hope is on the way
He is a Star that gives direction
the way to salvation
He is a Star that will lead me
to the Eternal place, His Kingdom
He is a Star, my starlight,
The Star of my life.

HOLINESS

My soul yearns for holiness
Being human, where are you?
Divinity?
Moments of truth
I witness
I welcome
Through openness
Struggling through
Compromise
Must I?

Consciousness
Cautiousness
Of the words
I say.
I need
Spiritual Guidance
To tame my tongue
To guide my thoughts
To guard my actions
Worthiness,
I pray!

THE PATHWAY TO HOLINESS

Staggering virtues must be attained
Actual deeds must be practiced
Graces from the Holy Spirit received
Indeed it's the pathway to holiness.
Everyday is a struggle,
Discernment is often used
For the pathway to holiness
Repentant hearts, pious acts
Prayerful attitude with a lot of gratitude
Faithfulness in every move
And humility in every encounter
Let's work on the pathway to holiness.

AFTER GOD'S OWN HEART

How great it is to know that we are
Created in GOD's Image
How wonderful to feel our GOD's love
How blessed are we to be in GOD's vineyard
Yes indeed we are after GOD's own heart.
In GOD's Presence we are secured
In His arm we feel His warmth
In His sight we are His flocks
Yes indeed we are after GOD's own heart.
Women as we are, loved by GOD
Women of faith as we are called
Serving You LORD, our sincere desire
Yes indeed we are after GOD's own heart.
After GOD's own heart is a blessed opportunity
After GOD's own heart is a reality
After GOD's own heart leads to eternity
Yes our dear LORD, be with us forever and
Be in your heart, after your own heart, Amen!

LIVING IN POVERTY

No one can ever tell
How a poor family feels
Until someone will be in their boat sailing
Then you'll say, "I understand how it is to be poor."
They sometimes miss meals
They sometimes starved to death
They don't have shelter to protect their skin
Living in poverty is a tragedy
In some countries like ours
There is an extreme living status
We have people very rich
And we have family very poor
But the poor families that live in squatter areas
Are happy with strong family bonding
They really enjoy simple living
Living in poverty with these people is a blessing
True enough it is a blessing to be poor
Two Beatitudes in the Bible says so,
"Blessed are the poor in spirit, for
theirs is the Kingdom of heaven"
Blessed are they who hunger and thirst
For righteousness, for they will be satisfied,"
So bless the poor and the victims of hunger
that they may have peace in their hearts
Bless us all LORD, for the abundance and protection
It is indeed a true blessing, living in poverty.

SPIRITUAL JOURNEY

You travel far you travel near
Enjoying the sight-seeing
You take pictures, you buy souvenirs
from every place you have been
You go in groups, you go by yourself
You give time and save for the trips
You are engrossed seeing beautiful places
You need a break, indeed you need
There's a trip you need not spend
Just try to experiment, think about it.
It is through walking and talking with
this Traveler and He will be your
best Tour Guide ever.
First, He will teach you to forgive, not
to reserve a fare ticket
He will teach you to be humble, not to gamble
He does not have a travel book
but He will lead you to read the Bible.
When you travel with Him, no luggage to take
because He will take away your excesses
He will help you carry your loads
the burden that you have, will be in His hands
You don't need to buy any souvenirs
he will give you a lot of free gifts
No post cards, no brand name bags, nor credit cards.
instead, there is the faith, humility, wisdom at hand.
Why not start preparing yourself
to welcome your New Companion?
Have a free ride on the palm of His Hand
travel with Him in the right pathway
On the road He will show you the right from wrong.
He will protect you from harm and storm
He will provide you with all your needs
Just trust your Traveler, He will keep you
company in your Spiritual Journey.

SPIRITUAL REALITY

You are at the end of the long line
You are busy with your life
You don't have time to spare a moment
To walk and talk with a friend
He invited you to visit
Once a week in His temple
You only go as you wish
And don't finish the service.
You see the Holy Eucharist exposed
You just do the sign of the cross
You go to confession once in a blue moon,
But you also go and receive Holy Communion.
You always watch the television
You don't have a prayer time set,
You read your daily horoscope from the paper
You are not aware that the Bible exists.
One morning when you woke up
You can't breathe and almost call 911
You thought you were going to die
Then, you called GOD to bail you out
GOD is at your side all the time
Willing to ransom you at any moment
He just want to be closer to you
For you to know about His Son JESUS
Nice to know we are still breathing
And still entitled to a gift of life
GOD calls you now so grab the chance
It's never too late to be His servant.
So you're no longer at the end of the long line
You're not busy with your life anymore
You have all the time to walk and talk with Him
That is Spiritual Reality, the start of your
Spiritual Journey.

SPIRITUAL HOSPITALITY

It's a great day today, I may say
In my heart it says, "Thank You LORD
for Your greatness."
The beauty of nature I admire, I reclaim
the wonders of GOD is everywhere.
Everyday I couldn't help but to smile
for the radiant rays of the sun on my face
O LORD, it thrills me just to think I'm alive
to witness Your wonders, to appreciate
the gift of life.
The people I see, the strangers I meet
The friends that I talk to on a daily basis,
They are all Your gifts to me O LORD
It helps my well-being and my spiritual growth.
I welcome these gifts O LORD in my heart
they show me how it is to shape my life
LORD, thank You for the Spiritual hospitality
that the Holy Spirit have implanted in me
The Spirit of listening is a powerful tool
The beauty of listening is a self-discovery
The effect of listening is a Spiritual Hospitality
I will give my full attention, whenever it needed be.
What does it take to be hospitable?
Is it a welcome hand? Or welcome ears?
Or is it a welcome note? Or a welcome heart?
Be open and wait for the grace of
"Spiritual Hospitality."
LORD GOD, thank You for this wonderful gift.

SPIRITUAL CONNECTION

You are here, they are there and GOD
is everywhere
It is amazing how the LORD works
in mysterious ways
He touches people, He calls His creation
He is with you and me with
Spiritual connection.
He gives us strength, He fulfills promises
He watches your mother, father,
sisters and brothers
He guides your nieces, nephews and
in-laws as well,
He guarantees one thing, connecting us
with our kin
Spiritual connection is what He is providing
to communicate in silence and
through meditating
There is peace in our hearts, just to think
we are connected
The feeling is stronger, there is spiritual bonding
The joy that we feel in our hearts is real
To know that our loved ones are safe somewhere
safe in the Hands of GOD, a real protection
Blessing us always and granting the
Spiritual Connection
So let us trust the LORD for this wonderful gift
to be connected not only with our kin,
but with Him
Keep your faith and belief, to go on
with your lives
Let us be content for we are spiritually connected.

IN DARKNESS

We live in the world of beauty
We appreciate the nature around us
We see from our eyes different movements
We are lucky, we are able to see things.
Let us honor the blind for their hearts,
for their hope and perseverance, too
They only see things from their hearts
darkness, they don't even know how it looks.
Gloomy weather, heavy burden and feelings
signs of hopelessness and helplessness
feelings of shrinking and passing through tunnel
unpleasant, negative, destructive, that's darkness.
In the beginning of creation, light and darkness
were created, and they were also separated for
certain reason
All these were GOD's accomplishments in six days
The day and night that He created, He was pleased
The first couple did have a bright life
until they were tempted and committed a sin
That was then, the start of darkness
and sin was the manifestation of living in the dim.
We see the sun at daytime, so radiant
We see the stars and the moon at night, so brilliant
We can appreciate the brilliance in darkness
and that's how you should take darkness in your life
In your aloneness, loneliness and lowliness
In the darkness of your life, just watch for the rays
of the light in which within your reach
It is GOD who brightens your day and your way
No more darkness and no more dimness
Let the peace and calmness surround you
Always think that GOD is always there
to shine us through the darkness, too
We are waiting in the darkness, longing for the light
We are reassured of the light of CHRIST JESUS
The light of JESUS will come into the world
to guide us and lead us to the Kingdom of GOD.

IF . . . IS ONE POWERFUL WORD

Do you have a lot of *ifs* in your life?
Have you fulfilled all your *ifs?*
Are there more ifs hiding at your back?
If you can fulfill all those *ifs*, would
you be satisfied?

If I didn't ask questions about *if,*
will you know its value?
If I ask you more about facts of life,
will you respond?
Are you ready for these pertinent
queries of *ifs?*

If there are no planes and ships,
can we cross-countries?
If we don't have complete faculties,
can we function well?
If there is no oxygen, can we breathe?
If only you can fly, would you do it?

We need the *ifs* in our lives to keep us going.
We depend some of our goals and plans
on the *ifs*.
We have to make the *ifs* as our foot-rule,
Because the if gauges the success
of our future.

The common sense says, "the power of
If is, in the cause and effect."
Our decisions depend on how *if* is effective.
So from now on, let us be discreet in
Our choices,
May it be major or minor options.

Come to think of it, *if* we are not in this
world, where will we be?
If GOD didn't create mankind and all kinds
whom He will create?
Our GOD is an awesome GOD, creating
everything, non-living and human beings.
He even gave us the will to choose,
between good and evil.

So my dear readers, allow yourself
to exercise your *"if"* power,
In everything you do, in your waking-up
and your resting time.
In your choosing of friends and in your
service to GOD.
And even in your little ways of saying things.
If you have the chance to live just in short
time, what would you do?
Think about it!

THE SAINTS

Ordinary people they are
Doing extraordinary things
Extending a mile and afar
These are the people called, "Saints".
Persecution they suffered,
Humiliated at times;
Offered their lives for others,
These are the people called, "Saints."
Meditation and reflection
These they often do,
Mystical in their ways,
These are the people called, "Saints."
Life of mortification
Massive fasting and hermit's life,
Denial of oneself surrendering
Everything to GOD;
These are the people called, "Saints."
The way to Sainthood is not easy,
But with GOD's grace and with our
Pure intentions,
We will be walking on the road smoothly
So let's imitate our LORD JESUS,
For this is the perfect way to Sainthood.
Everyone is called to be a saint
So let us work hard to attain it
Let us invest a good amount of time
In transforming our lives
For in the future we'll be joining the
Rests of the saints.

THE CENTURION CREED

In every liturgical mass we always hear
these wonderful phrases
"LORD, I'm not worthy to receive You,
but only say the Word and I shall be healed."
These were uttered by an ordinary man,
the Centurion, with such strong conviction
and unconditional faith.
Yes, we are not worthy because of our
sinfulness
We are not worthy because of our pride
We are not worthy for we have our
unclean heart
But with the Body and Blood of our
LORD JESUS CHRIST, that we received
we are reassured of our worthiness.
So let us glue in our hearts the Centurion Creed.
Let us be repentant and be humble
for only in GODs grace that we would be healed.
Thank You LORD for Your Word,
in JESUS name, Amen!

FEAR

Frantic, feeling uncertain, fear of the unknown
Feeling isolated, suspicious at times . . . FEAR!
It is difficult to understand to have this kind of feeling
Reaching out, telling someone, must I?
Take a deep breath, drink a glass of water
It helps alleviate and minimize the fear
Constantly converse with someone
It helps divert your attention
If you focus your mind to something constructive
And need to know more and how?
Just open your Bible and pick out any Scripture
Ponder on that till you feel good and settled.
Fear of height, fear of darkness, fear of water,
Fear of flight
Phobias is the term at the end of each fear
Everyone is a victim of phobia of some sort
Handling this uneasy feeling takes some courage
The question to ask is, why are we scared?
Does it run in the family? Or just the environment?
Do we lack exposure to such object of fear?
FAITH is the answer, and we must have it.
But one interesting thing to know about fear is . . .
There is a Biblical message or Scriptural passage
that says, "The fear of the LORD, is the beginning
of knowledge."
So the fear that you feel is indeed constructive.
We can overcome any fear that will cross our way
We only have to trust GOD and have Faith,
for nothing is impossible with GOD's grace
fear is just temporary and we can deal with it!
Fear Not! GOD always says, "Fear Not!"

WALK THE TALK

Let us read the following Scriptures from the Bible
That will lead us to understand the essence of this poem.
It is about to walk the talk of the Good News,
To practice what you have learned and preached.

In Romans 10, chapters 14 and 15, it says,
"But how can they call on Him in whom they have
believed, and how can they believe in Him whom
they have not heard, and how can they hear without
someone to preach, and how can they preach unless
they are sent? As it is written, "How beautiful are
the feet of those who bring the good news."

It is indeed very clear what the Bible says
So let us put into action our transformation
Let us start changing ourselves from the inside
to be aware of what we say, think and act.

There is a saying about not putting into act
what you heard, that anyone who has heard
the words, but not put into practice, is like
the man who built his house on the ground
without foundation;
So to have a sturdy foundation, start the evangelization.

Everyday we are given a chance to share the gospel
in meeting strangers and whomever we may encounter
we can start at home, in our workplace, anywhere
Be reminded constantly that we can be models
of humanity.

Be a good listener and be tender in your care
Be humble in your undertakings
Be polite, approachable, gentle and sweet
These virtues are weapons for effective
evangelization.

You don't need to have a title or a position
to share the Good News
Be as you are, a child of GOD, precious in His eyes
Continue to ask GOD's grace for everything
you do and say especially the spreading of
His Word to help you walk the talk.

I thank You our Almighty for Your Word and
the wisdom that You have given Your humble
servants and help us constantly walk the talk
Grant us the grace to know the Bible through
reading from our hearts, and guide us
everyday and all the way through, Amen!

LIFETIME

There is a time for everything
There is a time for everyone
A time for span of life
A lifetime to ponder.

Ecclesiastic verses meet our needs
Putting us in the proper place
Routine tasks, part of lifetime activities
Lifetime not guaranteed, but exists.

Awareness of lifetime
And carefree at times
So treasure precious moments
and every bit of it
Life is too short, don't make
it shorter
Lifetime is only a time
But life is essential.

So make use of lifetime wisely
Grab all the virtues you can have
Ask our Almighty to give you the grace
the grace of living your life fully.

Have A Good Life With GOD's Love!

DECISION

"To be or not to be", that is the question
An ancient and famous Shakespeare's quotation
To do or not to do is another question to ask
That needs an answer but no where to find.
The certain and uncertain, both needs to be chosen
Always in between two major decisions
Positive or negative, black or white
Choices to make and no alternatives.
The common phrases for the uncertain answers
are, "maybe," "perhaps," "it's up to you," or "I'll see."
The answers that are certain and sure thing,
are, "yes," "no," "I'm positive," "I'll do it," or "I'll go."
It's difficult sometimes to just say "no," or resist.
It's easy to say "yes," and no hassle.
Sometimes you need to decide critically.
So the definite solution must always be ready.
When you wake up in the morning
What do you do the first thing?
You don't know if you'll drink coffee or not?
Shall I go to work, or call in?
Shall I stop deciding and just go with the flow of the day?
Decision, decision, decision, is always on the way.
Now, let us see what the Scripture says about decision.
When JESUS CHRIST called His disciples, there
was no "but" and no "doubt," they *immediately* followed
JESUS without hesitancy, another word was, "*at once*," and
they followed Him truly.
The amazing thing in knowing CHRIST JESUS and the
Holy Spirit, is even in our daily decision, we will be
empowered and guided
The gift of discernment will be given and received,
if you asked for it
So let me ask you this, "Are you still deciding to follow
JESUS? (Just ponder on His Word, the decision is yours!)

TOAST TO THE MEMORIES

May the childhood times bring joyous experience
May the school days give smooth adjustment
May the graduation moments be memorable
The moments during the prom most of all.
The challenging college life starts
Here's to the mature life level
Many precious moments to treasure
More of challenges to have faced
Wonderful people meet along the way
Here's to the fruitful experience.
Toast to the memories is like a eulogy
honoring the past, the people you love
preparing yourself, then for a better future
Continue to toast to the memories
Work on your "better" tomorrow,
But toast to your now, while there's still time,
to express your gratitude, appreciation,
Acknowledgement and recognition,
of Who made you, "you."
Ponder on the thoughts of Whom we should
offer our toast.
Toast to the memories of the Maker of the
past, the future and the present.
Toast to GOD's vivid memories of our lives.

NUMBERS

Numbers are short cuts
for communicating something
They are signs and symbols
that characterize certain words.

911 is for emergency code
It's all over the States,
even the kids know
Telephone codes are varied
411 for directory assistance
0, is for the operator.

More number codes for the
telecommunications
It only shows numbers are
essential in this world.
even in the Bible there is a
significant number
7, a perfect and famous one
symbol of completion.

In the Bible we have the Book
of Numbers.
It's one of the Pentateuch
Pentateuch is the first 5 Books
in the Bible, the Genesis, the
Exodus, the Leviticus, the
Deuteronomy are the other 4.

40 is another important number
in the Bible
40 days in Noah's time the flood stays
40 days our LORD JESUS fasts and
contemplates as human
And after each generation, 40 years
apart until JESUS was born.

There are common numbers used
in this modern world,
143 is a short cut for "I love you,"
Then, there is 24/7, the latest one
means, non-stop, all the time or
all day long, as in 24 hours.

Let me share with you my
experience about numbers,
it started when I was in school age
I didn't like number 6 ever since
Guess what? I realized now that in the
Book of Revelation 666 is an omen.

Numbers, just like the letters convey
meanings and messages,
and just remember from day one means
"In the beginning"
The story of creation started, then GOD
counts everyday, staggering His creations
and on the 7th day (the final day), He rested
and was pleased with everything He created.

But, let us focus on the significant truth
that there is 1 GOD and no else, we have
10 Commandments to guide us in our lives
And we will be guided by the Holy Triune

So, 143 LORD and we know that You are there
in our lives 24/7.

GOD IS ENOUGH

We are in this world to live and die
We ought to know the how and why.
We have our conscience to follow through
But do we really know what to do?

We question ourselves and wonder at times
On how we can survive the daily tasks
But we always forget that no matter what
GOD IS ENOUGH, we should remember that.

Yes GOD is enough and the enough answer
To all the doubts and personal concerns
All we have to do is to acknowledge His Presence
Then the contentment and peace will be there.

Yes GOD IS ENOUGH and His love stands out
His love is enough to hold on tight
GOD IS ENOUGH and we should know that
So let's start putting our GOD in our hearts
To be the first and not our last.)
Again, GOD IS ENOUGH . . .

THE NOW

"Live one day at a time," our motto should be in life
Think of now and never to dwell on yesterday
Be better today than yesterday
Be better tomorrow than today
Do the best you can and make the most of it
You can glance at the rear view mirror, when
you're driving a car, and it means you can only
recall your past from time to time.
If you want to change for a better, you should do
it now or never and grab the chance, without hesitation.
Opportunity knocks only once in a while
Memories trigger your mood
Memories are not current
Live not in memories, live in now.
You don't know what's tomorrow
Tomorrow might never come
You can plan ahead for the whole year
But GOD Has plans for everyone including the now
So be healthy now and live wisely
Serve humanity, serve your family
and serve the LORD most of all.
Whatever you do today is rewarding
because you're working on your sturdy future
The future is tomorrow, the past is yesterday
Whatever you say, do, and think now,
do it to the fullest
Be at peace with everyone, with yourself and
with our Creator.
He will show you the way to now and here,
then to Eternity.

THE MOMENT OF TRUTH

Let me tell you a short story
About a Great Guy who is honest
He tries to show His friends how
He loves and cares for them.
He is with the twelve friends and
they go around towns to tell the
people the Good News
This Great Guy is a doctor
He heals and cures the mentally ill
and takes away the pains of the injured
He tells great moral lessons while
He is treating the town people,
He teaches them a lot of things
including the laws and decrees.
One day, a group of envy people find out
about this Great Guy, now famous in town
Let's call this people, "Curious Group"
and let us see what they want.
First, they don't believe in the doctor's ability
Second, they accused Him of malpractice
and breaking the law
Then, they even made stories about His
reputation, "all not true."
The Doctor was punished for all His deeds
The leader of the "Curious" group hired
someone to spy on Him and paid Him
a bagful of greed.
But the hired person, let's call him, "Twelfth"
is one of the doctor's friends

It really hurts to witness this kind of betrayal.
"Twelfth" told the leader of the Curious group
that whomever he embrace and whom he'll
give a kiss, is the doctor indeed, the One
Who is doing the great deeds.
So the moment of truth is at hand
that the doctor in captive is destined to die
Just imagine for a simple but hypocritical kiss
His life is in danger
The moment of truth has come and He faces
the accusers
This story is endless, to continue if you wish
instead of the doctor's story, it's the story of
The Real Savior, none other than CHRIST JESUS
It's now the moment of truth. Truth about
The Divine Redeemer, that JESUS is the TRUTH!

THE FIRST GIFT

Did you ever know what the first gift is?
Why don't we ponder for a while and dig
a little bit?
It is indeed true what the Bible says
about this Wonderful baby laid down
on the hay
The first gift we received is none other
than our LORD JESUS, who was born
to save us.
It is the very first gift as says in John3:16
"For GOD so loved the world that He gave His
only Son, so that everyone who believes in Him
might not perish, but might have eternal life."
So let us treasure this precious first gift
For this is the best gift a mankind can ever have
Everyone on this earth has received the
First Gift, and we thank our LORD GOD for
giving the whole nation the gift of salvation
So remember now that the Child to be born on the
25th of December, is the gift, The First Gift, ever.

RECIPE FOR LOVE

On this fourteenth of February
I have a wonderful gift "a love recipe"
So if you want to receive the recipe
for love, you have to be attentive
and follow it carefully.

First, you have to prepare your two
hands to embrace
and hug the family members with grace
Then, tell them the three words, "I love you"
and tell them that you care for them, too.

When your spouse is hurt and you want
to say sorry, flowers and chocolates
must also be handy
Don't let the heartaches lingered overnight
Don't go to sleep without patching-up.
The following love ingredients must be added
compassion, understanding and obedience
Mix all these ingredients and stir them well,
You'll come out with a delicious and perfect meal.

This recipe has been handed from
generation to generation
It is accessible to all GOD's creation
The power of love is there all the time
Valentine's Day or not, love is in our hearts
Because GOD loves us no matter what
"Agape" it is called, a love that is
Unconditional, a LOVE that is for all of us.

RECIPE FOR GENEROSITY

Let us prepare the ingredients for a recipe
A recipe that was discovered recently
It is about mixing of virtues together
To come up with a recipe for generosity.
Start with 10% tithing to your church
Or to any congregation you belong
Then, have two open hands to offer a service
to the community and neighborhood calls.
Open a packet of that talent wrapped
Share it to the people around
Chop all your vanities in life
because a lot of virtues is at hand
to be used at random.
Gather your clothes and belongings
hand them to the needy and indigent
Stir all virtues gently
And you will have a recipe for generosity.
GOD knows what's in our hearts
And He knows that we are part of the
ingredient at large
So are you ready to serve this new recipe
A Recipe For Generosity?

RECIPE FOR HUMILITY

Prepare a frying pan for the pride on the run
Buy a pleasant attitude mix on the bun
Make sure to bend that high pride, it's no fun
The pride must be fried under the sun.

In order to have a tasty and nutritious food
The food for thoughts for us all
We have to know the secret of the menu
The ingredients for the pride to swallow.

Take a hug full of honesty and warmth
Mix it with cheerful smile a genuine one
Then, admit a handful of mistakes
And ask an ounce of forgiveness.

After giving up your pride to oblivion
Look for the appetizer for reconciliation
Start distributing the recipe of humility
Let the Best Cook taste the recipe,
The Almighty!

RECIPE FOR KINDNESS

Everyone can be a chef for kindness
Just follow the following recipe
And you got it made.
First, you must be willing to be kind
or else, the ingredients won't be completed
Let us now start following the recipe
step by step: Number one, you must ask
100 percent of GOD's grace
then, followed by fractional doses of
Random Act of Kindness
Have a tablespoon of keen observation
Alertness of what's in your surrounding
Look for the opportunity to serve, with
a glassful of willingness.
Be ready with 7 slices of compassion
Mix with the 2 hands of hug and embrace
A touch of warmth and maybe a tight shake hands
And pour a lot of smile and laughter
Then, stir every ingredient with a generous heart
Now you made a very enticing appetite
Serve the food of kindness to the community
And don't keep the recipe a secret, pass it on please.

KINDNESS . . . IT IS

Do everything in this world your best
GOD will take care of the rest
Include doing a lot of "Random Act
Of Kindness",
You'll be rewarded at the end.
Because you started a great beginning.

It is worth your time to extend another mile
And doing things with a great smile
Practice the act of kindness randomly
Your life will be changed, it's a guaranty.

There are tremendous surprises in this life
One of them is unexpected reward
The blessings and graces that we have
All these come from our LORD, our GOD.

From now on, let's cultivate more virtues
For virtues are weapons in our daily use
Let's start now by being kind
And start praying any given moment
Ask GOD for the grace of kindness
Kindness . . . it is, it is granted.

SET THE CAPTIVES FREE

"Set the captives free," as says in the Bible
from the bondage of slavery, self-destruction
and human wills
We need to free ourselves from these
undesirable things
Freedom it is, freedom we need to have.

The history speaks a lot of slavery
The Exodus says about the departure
of the Hebrews, the fleeing from Egypt
led by Moses and discourse took place
between the Egyptian and Hebrew leaders.

Pharaoh, the Egyptian leader didn't let go of
the Jews from his hand, so GOD sent
Moses to take them out from their land.
The departure took a long journey to the
Promised land and Moses fought hard to let
the Israelites out.

Another set of leaders were justice defenders
one of them was President Lincoln, who was
against slavery
Freedom of speech, freedom of press, freedom
of religion and freedom of suffrage
Now we can express ourselves and not be scared.

Another freedom that is important to remember
is the freedom of confession, to GOD and to
whomever you want to confess to,
there would be peace and inner healing in
sincere confession and the heaviness that you
carry would be lessened.

The Holy Spirit can change the captivity to
different gifts:
The freedom from stubbornness to the
gift of obedience
The freedom from doubt to the gift of faith
The freedom from anger to the gift of calmness.
The freedom from loneliness to the gift of joy
The freedom from hate to the gift of love
The freedom from pride to the gift of humility
The freedom from confusion to the gift of peace.

Just imagine the freedom that our Almighty is
giving us
He gives the freedom to choose, between
good and evil
He shows His love and mercy and gave His Son
The gift of freedom we attained from the
Sovereign One.

When GOD calls us, it is indeed a package deal
He guides us every step of the way
Peace is the bottom line in all our struggles
Freedom is the front line, our wings to GOD's
Eternal Kingdom.

THE DANCE OF LIFE

Let us sing a song that pleases our LORD
Let us proclaim His wondrous deeds
Let us celebrate His awesomeness
Let us dance with the music that GOD
Has planted within us.

The songs and psalms that we learn
from the Book of David, the prophet
are the songs that lift our hearts
to the promise and joy of salvation.

Let us worship the LORD our GOD
Let us rejoice and be glad
Let us celebrate the dance of life
The dance that tuned-in with GOD's
melody of love.

ONE ON ONE

What is one on one?
Is it a number put together?
Does it involve more than one person?
One on one is a way of communication.
What is one on one?
Is it a confrontation?
Is it a conjecture for reconciliation?
One on one is a session between two persons.
One on one is a healthy way to commune
with each other, a holy way to approach
a brother and a sister.
It is a pathway to a better relationship
our intimate and deep relationship
With our LORD JESUS.

A DAY TO REMEMBER

Some days are days to be worthy of pondering
Some days are days to look forward to
Some days are not essential at all,
But a day to remember is a day to remember.
Every year we have days to celebrate
The beginning of the year, the New Year's Day
Then, back a month, it is a Day of Christmas
Second month of the year, the month of the heart
Cultural celebration is almost every month
And every month, there is a celebrant
It could be a birthday, anniversary or anything
But a day to remember, is a day to remember.
There is day for a mother and a day for a father
There is a day for the workers everywhere
There is a day for the President and a day for
the soldiers
But a day to remember, is a day to remember.
There is a day to remember, a significant one
It is a day that no one knows when it'll come
It is a day to meet every being and the Sovereign One
It is the final day, the Judgment Day!
Yes, it is a day, a day to remember.
So let us prepare and do something
Let us treasure the lives that we are given
Let us be vigilant in every step we make
Let us not forget this day, a day to remember,
A Day To Remember! is only a reminder.

OVER-COMER

It's indeed true that GOD won't give us
things we can't handle, for he teaches us to
be an over-comer.

GOD is always there, in tribulations
He guides us every step of the way
He shows the way to be an over-comer.

So stop complaining, stop the blaming
Start trusting, start believing
These are the steps to overcoming.

Be an over-comer and ask GOD for the graces
Have a strong faith and believe that you
can handle the trials, for you are an over-comer.

Be proud of yourself, of your accomplishments
All these graces that are from GOD Himself
So from now on be an over-comer yourself.

Over-comer you become, faith you hold on
GOD is your strength and don't forget
Our LORD JESUS is the best over-comer of all.

BE YOURSELF

It is difficult to cope
But there's always hope
Don't be a dope
Be yourself, yap or nope?

You always worry
Don't be sorry
Don't be fury
Be yourself, be merry.

You are protesting
You're complaining
You're procrastinating
Be yourself, that's the thing.

You're a giver
You're not a taker
It's not fair
Be yourself, it does matter.

Be yourself all the time
Don't pretend to be someone else
Be honest and be human
Because you're always in
GOD's Hands

Whatever you do
Whatever you say
Whatever you think
Be yourself remember
You're created in GOD's Image.

THE GIFT OF LIFE

Nothing is free in this world
An adage that we know about
Everything has a price
Including our way of life.

But life itself is free
It is given by our LORD GOD
The miracle of life it is
Since the time of Adam and Eve.

The thing that is puzzling
Is the rampant killing
Murdering of the unborn child
Who will be a future sibling.

"Life is too short", I always say
Don't make it shorter even a day
Enjoy the gift that GOD Has given
The gift of life, even beyond
Which is, "The Eternal Life".

LORD, thank You for the gift of life.

PEACE

The stillness of the night is a great moment
The calmness of the ocean, the sound of silence
The twinkling stars, the radiance of the moon
The shadow and silhouette on earth is prominent.
In this world there is a lot of chaos and confusion
War exists between nations, feud among families
Anger, hatred, anxiety and fears and more
We are in the verge of losing ourselves
We create our own problems with wrong attitudes
We can't handle situations properly, no diplomacy
We blame others, we don't acknowledge own mistakes
That's how we live our lives in this chaotic earth.
We try to solve our own problems our ways
We always depend on our human instincts
We justify and reason out for every wrong doings
We think we are happy and contented.
Peace is a magical word and difficult to achieve
Because we are not willing to surrender
everything to Him, the Almighty
Let's give up the vanities, and obsessions in life
So we can attain the peace we deserve to have.
We can only find peace through GOD's grace
We have to look deeper inside us, to see what we have
We have these gifts from the Holy Spirit
The gift of peace, the gift of contentment, the gift
of calmness and the gift of inner healing.
Peace is a powerful gift and it takes care of a being
It will teach us to forgive and to forget as well
To have peace in our hearts is a great virtue
So forgive and forget, the gift of humility is at hand
P- then is to pardon others and yourself
E- is to embrace your hurt, embrace JESUS
A- is accepting one's sins and confess them
C- is for contentment after a good confession
E- is for Eternal Kingdom, that is awaiting for us
wherein Eternal Peace can be found. Amen!

EMBRACE YOUR HURT, EMBRACE JESUS

When you're hurt and seems it's endless
Close your eyes and think of JESUS
Ponder on Him on the cross
And contemplate on His passion
The hurt and persecution He suffered on earth
The physical pain and the five wounds He attained
LORD JESUS, thank You our Savior
For loving us so deeply without stain.
When you're alone and feel so weary
JESUS is there to say, "Don't worry",
Just remember Him that He is human
Embrace JESUS and hold Him in your heart.
When your burden seems so heavy, always
remember the gift of JESUS that come in handy
The gift of suffering, the gift of redemption
Let us ask JESUS the grace of endurance
for our salvation.
When you're in pain and can't forgive
It's even hard to imitate JESUS, for He says,
we need to do it, seventy times seven,
LORD JESUS, we need the grace to forgive
and be forgiven, in JESUS name.
When your world seems to end
Hang in there! Hold on tight!
What is there? What is to hold? It is JESUS
to embrace and His promise of salvation.
When you're down, lonely and feeling alone
Just keep still and know that JESUS is there
What a wonderful feeling, a real assurance
that our LORD is always present.
When you started feeling good and feel the joy
It's because you surrender everything to Him
You embraced your hurt and you embraced JESUS
Thank You LORD for being there, our Mighty Savior!

DENIAL

You are in the middle of turmoil
Your mind is somewhere else
You are carefree
You are in denial.
Denial is a response
Denial is a defense mechanism
Denial is a no concern of what's
going around
Denial is one of the stages
of grieving
It counteracts the ill-feeling
It is a temporary relief
It is a pretention of "as if".
There is a denial that is positive
A denial that we can learn from
A denial that will lead us to
transformation
It is a denial that is in Scripture
Our LORD JESUS emphasized
the importance of denial
It is a denial of oneself
And a command to follow Him
It is a detachment from the
material world
It is the start of imitating JESUS
So denial it is . . . let's wisely use it.

THE LAST OF THE LASTS

What could it be in a person's mind at the
verge of the approaching death?
I like to get into their minds now.
I heard:
"I'm prepared"
"I don't care"
"I wish to live longer"
"Where will I go?"
"I don't want to go to hell"
"Is there a purgatory?"
"Heaven would be wonderful"
"Thank You LORD for my transformation"
"I just wish I made the difference"
"I will miss my loved ones"
"GOD please forgive me"
"I don't deserve this"
"Thank You, I'm ready"
"Will you give me another chance?"
"Enough is enough"
"Pain is unbearable"
"Pain is worthy of my sacrifice"
"I know I will be with our Creator
very soon"
Last thought . . . I thought
Last wishes . . . I wish.
Last requests . . . granted.
Last rites . . . rites of penance
and reconciliation
Last moments . . . moments of truth
Last time . . . zero hour
Last person . . . myself
The last of everything is
GOD's Infinity

THE LAST JUDGEMENT

Prepare the way, we must
To work on earth for future investment
To live our life, the life of
the last judgment
The Holy Bible has a lot to tell
about the pathways to GOD's Kingdom
An invitation is there, ready for us
to seek and claim for our final freedom.
Charity begins in our hearts
Pathway to righteousness is at hand
Let's open our eyes for the chance
to see JESUS in everyone's face.
Life is too short
Let's live our life to the fullest
Always think today is our last day
So we'll know where we stand
In the last judgment.
Let's not be afraid to face the reality
Let's be repentant and forgiving
Let us rejoice and praise the Almighty
for He will guide us to Eternity
The last judgment is here in this world
It's just a matter of what to choose
So let us ask GOD's grace to lead us
to the path where the angels mingle,
to our final destination, the Kingdom
of Heaven
The Last Judgment it is . . . Fear not!

A REASON TO LIVE

Created in GOD's Image, a reason to live
GOD Has plan for everyone, a reason to live
A time to be born, a reason to live
To love GOD above all, a reason to live
To love your neighbor and yourself,
a reason to live
To serve GOD and mankind, a reason to live
To receive the gifts of the Holy Spirit
a reason to live
We are called to be Saints, a reason to live
We are here on earth, most of all
to work on our way to the
Kingdom of Eternal Life
an authentic reason to live.

SLOW BUT SURE

Have you tried to observe a turtle around you?
A slow movement they show, but sure of what they do
This is what we need to follow through
The slow pace it is, but aiming the best.
Many investors and scientists tried this motto
and most of them are successful, too
"Rome wasn't built in a day," as the adage says,
So, take things one at a time, and you got it made
When your life starts to change, from good to
better, that's the way to transform,
a staggering motion, the right pathway
So move slowly and divinely, for your
Spiritual conversion is on the way truly
"slow but sure," surely GOD knows
that the Holy Spirit is with everyone and
freely He flows.

A BEAUTIFUL HEART

There's a "Beautiful Mind",
A title of a movie
A story of a mentally ill individual
And let me tell you that there is
Beautiful Heart too, not in a movie,
But it's in everyone
Anything that a person says
Reflects who you are
Whatever you do, it says a lot about you
But the contents of your words
Are the results of your actions
It's the heart that speaks a lot
If you're kind in deeds and words
You do possess a beautiful heart
Generous of your service, extending
Extra miles, and with a ready smile,
You're not only have a beautiful heart
You also have a genuine heart
So be beautiful in all aspects
Especially, be heart-fully beautiful,
With your beautiful heart.

This poem was written a day after our Recollection with Fr. Joel. We had our monthly assembly and this was held during Holy Week. As the poem says, we were gathered in circle and reflected on our own concerns and we offered our reflections to our LORD JESUS while holding the crucifix.

REFLECTION UPON REFLECTION

We were gathered in circle sitting position, with candles lit in the middle of the floor, and lights were off and there was a sound of silence.
The passing of the crucifix started by the priest and poured out his utmost feeling while holding the wounded body of JESUS that was nailed to the cross. The crucifix was then handed to the next person, expressing her sentiments too, sobbing, thanking GOD for the healing and the miracles she claimed. This process of solemnity crucifix procession allows everyone to commune with the Almighty; to give witness to His kindness, goodness, and greatness; to humbly ask for forgiveness and to just pour each utmost inner selves.
We heard sisters who honestly expressed fear of being alone; women of faith who experienced loss of love ones; handmaids with illness that miraculously healed; some cancer survivors yet fear of its recurrence; Repentant daughters with transformed lives; also some with financial difficulties; humble servants with fear of uncertainties and fear of the unknown; mothers who are scared of the daily tasks especially being grandmas and those who expressed hurts and heartaches from friends betrayal and asking for the gift of forgiveness; wives asking for the wisdom and understanding in coping with the relationships with husbands and many, many more that only You LORD can grasp and understand.

O LORD JESUS, thank You for allowing us to have these moments with You and giving us inner healing and granting us your love, mercy and care. In Your Hands LORD, we commend our spirits and we offer to You our everything even our nothingness.
All this I offer and pray to You in Your Mighty name and with the intercession of the Women of prayer warrior, the most Blessed ever Virgin our Mother Mary and with the constant companion, our Advocate the Holy Spirit, Amen!

LEADERSHIP

To be a leader is to be strong in
one's own conviction
To be a leader is to have a wide
range of understanding
To be a leader is to have big
ears to listen and a warm
heart to welcome everyone
To be a leader is to be a
good model
To be a leader is to be fair
in every angle
To be a leader is to place
oneself in other people's shoes
to grasp the truth
To be a leader is to avail oneself
To be a leader is to know how
to delegate tasks
To be a leader is to have the door
open for suggestion and opinion
of the people around
To be a leader is to be respectful
of oneself and of others
To be a leader is to teach, to guide
and to have willingness to learn
To be a leader is to serve not to lead
to be humble servant like our LORD
CHRIST JESUS
Be a divine leader in this human world!

BLOWING HORN

Are you bothered when someone honks at you?
Do you blow horn if you needed to?
Or do you blow horn for tiny bit reasons?
Blowing horn is a language of vehicles in the streets.
Blowing horn is a warning to avoid mistakes
Blowing horn is a greeting to a newly wed
Blowing horn is an emergency sign, needs attention
Blowing horn is a request when you want to turn
Blowing horn is a demand for those who can't wait
Blowing horn is a reminder that your car has a problem
But blowing horn in ancient times is an announcement
A message by the prophet in the Old Testament
Blowing horn should be used properly
Don't abuse its purpose and don't use it frequently
Remember, people have their differences
So let us avoid putting ourselves in a mess
For at times miscommunication leads to mishap
For safety and peace of mind, minimize the honking
Always remember, our LORD is there guiding us
Wherever we are.

MONDAY! MONDAY! MONDAY!

First weekday of the week, Monday!
New beginning after the weekend, Monday!
Rush! Rush! Rush!, Monday!
Seven members of the family, one washroom,
Hurry up! Hurry up!, Monday!
Traffic heavy honking! Monday!
School bus stops every corner, Monday!
Postal cars, you see every few blocks, Monday!
Don't be late, be punctual, Monday!
Salespeople, don't make a call on Monday!
Be on the look out, your boss is at your back,
Monday!
Garfield, the famous cat character hates . . . Monday!
Don't blame your unpleasant moods on
your Monday "blues," Monday!
Overcome your Mondays, by thinking ahead,
By pretending it's Tuesday
Be positive and try singing,
Monday! Monday! Monday! . . .

BEFORE AND AFTER

Joy after sorrow
Triumphs after trials
Delight after distress
Smile after frowning
Gladness after sadness
Light after darkness
Kindness after cruelty
Compassion after apathy
Praising after cursing
Sweetness after bitterness
Diplomacy after rudeness
Orderliness after chaos
Peace after war
Reconciliation after forgiveness
Blessings after complaints
Calmness after turmoil
Humility after pride
Obedience after stubbornness
Truthfulness after deceit
Honesty after lying
Faithfulness after betrayal
Enlightenment after discouragement
Love after hatred
Generosity after greediness
Thoughtfulness after selfishness
Friends after feud
Inspiration after desperation
Transformation, conversion
"Metanoia"
Awakening at last!

A BOOKMARK

A Bookmark is just like a map
that tells where you're at
so you'll know where to go back
It'll tell you, too, how far have you
gone in your journey of reading.
You don't need to flip back
It is a small piece of paper, it might be
a single petal, or a favorite picture
It is light in weight, frequently used
It could be a fancy piece of metal
smooth edge, bronze, golden in color.
Bookmark is very useful to everyone
Don't fold the pages of your book
Handle it with care
for there is a bookmark handy
to keep you find the trail
Our life is just like a book
that needs to slow down,
flip in slow motion
page to page, phase to phase
We are marks in this world, until we
reach the final page of our life stage
So when you have a new book
make sure to have a bookmark to use.
Bookmark it is for the book
Life mark we are created in
"GOD's Image"

I BELIEVE

There are many poems written about, "I believe"
"I believe," tells a lot of things
It says about one's principle in life
It creates one's character.
Let me tell you what I believe in or what not
Let me express my opinion, it may make sense
And who knows, it might count
So you can or may believe it or not
I believe that, "Ripley's Believe It Or Not"
is believable, whether you like it or not
They spent time to search and study
for all the unbelievable scenes seen on the tv
I believe we are entitled to our own opinion
I believe "equality of rights," is in labor union
I believe you can tell anything you want
provided you hurt no one.
I believe in this world nothing is impossible
I believe it says in the amazing Book, "The Bible"
I believe we can handle our problems
I believe that we need to ask GOD's grace
I believe we can reach our goals
I believe it has proven many times on earth
I believe going to the moon is possible
before it happened
I believe in the power of knowledge
I believe that we are unique
I believe in myself so you should too
I believe "not" in fortune tellers
I believe in your ability, I believe in you
I believe most of all, that we are loved and blessed
I believe we are created in GOD's Image
I believe in One GOD the Almighty
The Father of Heaven and Earth
Thank You LORD for believing in us
And that I believe from my heart
So believe in the faith that you have
The faith of believing in GOD
Believe! Believe! Believe!

VIRTUES

Good qualities, positive attitude, if you
possess these, you're a success
You've been patient, you're honest
that's the way to run business
Caring for people, giving good service,
catering to the right prospects
Virtues of any kind, very useful every time.

Random act of kindness, grab it
any chance moments
You will feel good and you'll be respected
Humility is another virtue and it's the best
Peace is the reward of all the efforts
you have endured.

Let us practice all the virtues we have received
And let us apply them in our daily encounters
Our lives will be better for we
are on the right track
Rest assured that our LORD GOD is always
at our back

THANK YOU

"Thank you", two powerful words used for gratitude
To say these gracious words are spoken with the
right attitude, a "thank you" from the heart means a lot
A thank you that is whispered is sweet and gentle.
Thank you is part of everyday life and often used
And no one is exempted to utter these words
Just observe the number of times it's mentioned.
In twenty four hours it is indeed a daily use
Let us start from long time ago
A thank you from our parents when we were born
A thank you from us too for this wonderful gift of life
A thank you for the blessings and graces everyday
Even for what we called, coincidences and blessing
in disguise, they are the little miracles we encounter.
A thank you is enough to acclaim GOD's love
Our LORD is so understanding and a loving GOD
He knows we are appreciative of His wonderful works.
And He teaches us to be grateful and kind
He wants to see the smiles on our faces and say a
word of thanks
THINK ABOUT THIS:
We didn't ask for the wind, the sun, the moon and
the stars, the rain, the sea, the river and the ocean;
How about the mountains, the birds up high, animals
that crawl and all these wonderful creatures,
OUR LORD GAVE THEM ALL!
The materials in this world, He made them accessible.
the job, the luxuries, the people around, the friends
we call, also the challenges, the success, the fame,
the fortune and our goals are part of our daily
endeavors, aren't we thankful for those?

Once a year we celebrate the "Thanksgiving Day",
Won't it be nice to celebrate this event every moment
of our day, for as long as live we have our lives to
be thankful for, even beyond this life, there is
Eternal life to be grateful for.
With joyful hearts and praises, let us shout to the
LORD "THANK YOU FOR EVERYTHING!"

THE REAL WORLD

Wake-up reality is here
Routine tasks here we are again
Beating the traffic
Catching the bus or train
At work, stress is the name
Exchange of ideas
Exchange of words
Not uncommon in the workplace
Eight hours or more to finish
Stop at the grocery store
Buy something or buy foods
For the husband and the kids
The man in the family comes home
A salesman maybe or a mechanic
Maybe working in the warehouse?
Everyone is facing the routine
Everything is the same daily tasks
Different people from different
Culture and background
Same world
Same air
Same reality
"The Real World."

WILL YOU TAKE TIME?

In this chaotic world, we need to be reminded
there is beauty behind it.
So just relax and smell the fragrance of the
flowers, the green grass that symbolizes hope,
The different shapes of the leaves that sway
with the wind, and even the leaves that fall,
the natural colors of GOD's creations, the
different shapes of the clouds that form in
one's mind, the calmness of the river, the
brightness of the sun, the radiance of the moon,
the twinkling of the stars, the trees that give
shades, the breeze that you feel but don't see,
the pebbles that you step on, the rocks on the
ground and on the mountain tops, the rain that
is clear and with unique sound, the snow that
is so white and soft to touch and melt in your
hands, the thunder and the lightning that we
consider dangerous and yet needed to be
appreciated, the sea and the small ponds
(the home of the fish and other swimming
creatures like turtles (beautiful creatures
with unique features).
Now do you have time to ponder on these?
How much more of taking time you need
to see how beautiful you are and know why
GOD Has created you in His Image?
Remember GOD created everything just
in seven days.
So take few moments to ponder in your
heart the beauty within and behind, will you?

BEING A HUMAN

Flesh and blood our components
Sturdy bones, flexible muscles
Veins, arteries, run in the system
The human being is formed.

The thought process contains in the brain
The heart pumps, beat by beat
The skin is intact, the hair is grown
The human being is formed.

Words spoken, beauty seen, music heard
The humanity is a beauty
The gift of life, the power of love.
The miracles in life, come from our LORD.

So, let us be human in the real sense
Let's use our emotion and show compassion
Let us treat people humanly
By being divine in our humanity.

Humans we are, divinity we can do.

VISUAL SANCTUARY

I look up and see the sky and the radiant
beauty of the sun
The white clouds forming different shapes,
in a bluish-gray background,
the mallards, the small birds, the man-made
bird flying back and forth called airplane,
the sky's reflection in the water at the sea,
the ocean and the small ponds,
the peace I felt in my heart through my
visual sanctuary, the sky.

When the clouds turn dark, streaks of lightning
is obviously seen.
The thunder roars and loudly welcomes the rain.
No flying birds seen, they are on the hiding
waiting patiently for rain to stop pouring
I close my eyes and wait for a message from GOD
Peace still felt in my heart through my visual
sanctuary, the sky.

I am in the middle of a place called, "earth"
pondering, looking up waiting for the prompts
of the Holy Spirit
And I listen from my heart for the answer
to my prayers.
And through my visual sanctuary
I am receiving very clear the knock on my heart,
the voice that whispers telling me I am alright
with Him at my side.
Thank You my LORD for the gift of "visual
sanctuary" that I can talk to you any
moment of time.

REACTION FORMATION

Individual differences, reacts differently
Same situation given, choose
to be righteous
I just heard about, someone who wants
to ruin my reputation, getting mad?
Furious? Wanting to get even?
Why bother? Only GOD knows
what's in my heart?
I live with the holy ones, stoop on
vicious level?? Nope!
Thank you for the wisdom;
Transformation!
What to do with them?
The "I don't care" attitude people.
Offer a silent prayer, I did!
I'll do more!
React this way
GOD reacts with the prayers!
Bless us all LORD, forever!

WHAT SHOES ARE YOU WEARING?

It's nice to have lots of pairs of shoes
It's comfortable to wear sneakers
It's appropriate in Winter to wear boots
It's indeed important to wear something
on your feet.
Let's talk about the deeper meaning of
wearing shoes
The wearing of other shoes for example
Let's analyze the adage that says like this
"Put yourself in the shoes of other," and
you'll know how it is.
What we're dealing with is a figure of
speech actually, that helps us understand
the feelings of others really.
So always try to be in the shoes of others
It's always good to have "rule of the thumb"
and any rule for that matter.
It's always nice to be respectful of others'
feelings,
So would you want to try to wear shoes
not your size?
Will you feel awkward to wear loose or tight?
Will it matter, if it's really to know how it feels?
To be in a big or small size shoes?
So, from now on, let's be aware of our surroundings
and know the true language of wearing the other shoes
If you don't want to wear someone's shoes
you'll never know how and why that person's feel.
So, please at least try your best to fit in any shoes!

PRETENTIOUS DEATH

Pretending you're dying, what will you do?
Will you ask for forgiveness?
And will you forgive too?
Will you confess? Or protest?
Will you gather your family for reunion?
Or ignore their existence?
Will you start smiling?
Or continue to frown?
Will you pretend it's not happening?
Or will you accept it gracefully?
Pretentious death is a way to reality
It's a test
A practice
A preparation
So let's pretend that everyday is
our last day, so we can always
Be prepared.

I was inspired by Fr. Doug's homily on November 21, 2005. And the Gospel that day was from Luke 21:11, "There will be powerful earthquakes, famines, and plaques from place to place, and awesome sights and mighty signs will come from the sky."

FOCUS ON THE GOOD THINGS

We are in this world with a lot of challenges
We have to face the reality whatever it takes
We are at the verge of losing our grip
Why don't we focus on the good things?

Calamities of different sort are always
in the news
We have the earthquakes, the hurricanes
and the tornadoes
Not to forget the accidents, the crimes and
other mishaps
We really need to focus on the good things.

The war is still going on, indeed a national concern
There are family rivalries, feuds and broken homes
Terminal illnesses and the chronic diseases
Trigger our normal life and its essence
The more we need to focus on the good things.

We feel frustrated, depressed and stressed
of our daily routine tasks and activities
We are engrossed and overwhelmed with
our success
Still we don't have contentment and peace
Again, try to focus on the good things.

Esther B. Jimenez

The "good things" are not about the materials and fame
It is about the hope, the belief and the faith we have
It is about the coming of our CHRIST JESUS, our Savior
And His promise of our Eternal Salvation.

So, be not afraid of all the terrible things going on
Just focus on the good things and put this powerful
Verse (Luke 21:11) in your heart pocket
For you to ponder on at any given moment.

Let's pray for the people with Alzheimer's Disease and their loved ones. Constructive oblivion is when you forgive and forget. Destructive oblivion is when someone is victim of this agonizing illness, hiding from the back of one's mind.

OBLIVION

Tiny bubbles on the surface stays a while
"Now you see me, now you don't,"
A drifter on the run
Footprints on the sand
The waves run on them
Oblivion!
Unawareness, paying no attention
Ignoring small matters
Putting into the subconscious mind
Oblivion!
Love at first sight, sight blinded
By the self-centered ego trip
Not seen in moments, love forsaken
Oblivion!
Oblivion is a great weapon
Teamed with self-discipline
Humility is the great reward
Oblivion!
Forgetting the past, forgiving
Beautiful memories, hurtful events
Faces familiar, names forgotten
People with Alzheimer's Disease
Victims of tragic oblivion.
Oblivion will be in everyone
In each heart and in mind
An unknown time
Let's ponder on our LORD's passion
And never in oblivion we'll seek on
His Resurrection! Alleluia ! to the Risen LORD!

GENEROSITY

They say, "It is better to give than to receive,"
I say, "generosity" ranks the top in the list
Whatever you give and share, will come back
many folds, that is the, "the love and care."
So don't hesitate to give a second thought
to share your time, treasure and talent
to be a cheerful giver and not to expect
a thing in return,
and to be generous at any cost.
So let's ponder on the thoughts
on how our LORD CHRIST JESUS
gives His life, suffers for us
ransoms and forgives us as well.
So let's pause for a moment
and think of what we can do
to reciprocate the mercy and the love
that our LORD implants in our hearts.
So, LORD may You give us the grace
of generosity
And may You take us with You wherever
You may be, to be your servant O LORD
My Almighty!, Amen!

GETTING TO KNOW YOU

In the midst of nowhere, there is a chance to meet
a stranger
In the place that you know, you might meet a friend
In the everyday event there is someone watching you
In the middle of all these, is just a way of
getting to know you.
It's amazing how we are linked together
It's a wonderful feeling that someone indeed does care
It's a mystery that cannot be explained
Yes, it is GOD's own mysterious ways.
One of GOD's goals is to know you more
And to let you know that He is always there
He wants to be closer to us and be a friend
That's why He is getting to know all mankind.
So let us be open to our LORD's friendship
And be aware of His love, mercy and grace
Let us allow our LORD to know us more
And to have an intimate relationship with
His Son JESUS.
Once you get to know our LORD JESUS
And have an intimate relationship with Him
You will start feeling the peace in your heart
And you will have a friend to treasure forever.
So let's start getting to know our Friend
Let's trust, believe and have faith in Him
Let us surrender everything to the great King
Let's find out more about Him, shall we?
And acknowledge His plan for you and me
"Getting To Know You," is my desire my LORD
Thank You for I have received the gift of
knowing You, the everlasting gift of Eternity.

THE BLISS

In the silence of my heart
I feel the unexplainable uncertainty
The emptiness suddenly is filled
The fullness of life is experienced
Rejoice, joyful peace, the choice
Delight! Heavenly touch in every tinge
The wind gushed, seen the tears of joy
Aware! Carefree, ecstasy, trance
The moment of rapture alas! is here
The Presence of the Almighty
The Reality of His Existence
The Gifts of the Holy Spirit
Is upon us, within everyone
The bliss of life is here to find
The bliss of eternity is awaiting
The bliss is priceless, it is endless
It is in our hearts forever
Because we are created in GOD's Image.

THE LANGUAGE OF THE HEART

May it be verbal, may it be sign,
May it be silence, may it be eye contact
May it be by phone, or be by air mail
May it be by e-mail,
May it be young, may it be old
May it be female, may it be male
May it be single, may it be married
May it be a being of any nation,
May it be any profession
May it be animals, pets, or insects
May it be a handicapped
May it be perfectly healthy
May it be on the radio, or be in the tv
May it be you or may it be me
But most of all, it is our Creator
The Source of Wisdom
That connects us through the
"The Language Of Heart."

SOLILOQUY

Isolation, retreat, moments of solitude, soliloquy
This is the time that a person needs to
analyze oneself
Uncertainties, confusion, puzzled,
no direction to go.
Here is the moment, use it wisely, soliloquy.

In the stillness of the night, in the calmness
of the sea
In the brightness of the moon, in the twinkling
of the stars
All is great and conducive to ponder and think
Soliloquy, at last you can have it for yourself.

In soul searching, in meditating, in deep thinking
There is only one common thing, that is
to be in a place where serenity takes place
The solemnity of the space is inspiring.

You can pray and keep silent and contemplate
to feel the peace and contentment you never had
The Presence of GOD is what you need
Feel Him now and it is never too late.

In your moments of solitude, think of the
people you love
Ponder on how all of them contribute in your life
The Holy Spirit will guide you in your meditation
So just relax and have a full concentration.

The time of forgiveness works in time of stillness
You must forgive many times and each time,
you must forget
In your soliloquy, you'll discover the calmness
And in your heart, you'll be free of the resentments.

Take the chance of being alone to allow peace
in your heart
You have been waiting for so long for that moment
of silence
Not only peace you will have in your solitude
The Holy Spirit is generous to give you more.

Sometimes GOD Has messages for us
So try to be alone for a while and just listen
to His whispers
You might not hear His exalted Words, but you will
be moved by the Holy Spirit
And for all you know, you are already relaying
His messages.

So let us be still and know that He is GOD
to feel His Presence, His care, His mercy and love.
Let us find in ourselves the peace that we need,
The peace in our hearts, in our soliloquy with GOD.

BIRTH VS. DEATH

From womb to tomb, the life span
New life comes into the world
The gift of life freely given
The miracle happens, it's amazing.

Growth processes, development starts
Environment takes a big part
in the growing process of life
Family involvement is also important.

You can ask yourself
What's the use of life?
We're born in this world
to die in the long run.

Birth and death are compatible
There is a specific time for each one
Welcome into this world for birth
Good-bye from the earth for death.

Enjoy the gift of life, that GOD Has given
But let us prepare our way to heaven
The miracle of life, the mystery of death
both are included in GOD's great plans.

NEVER DOUBT

The Holy Spirit is within you, never doubt
The love and mercy within reach, never doubt
The guidance and protection are there, never doubt
GOD Has a plan for everyone, never doubt.

Never doubt, a single drop
Never doubt, a moment time.
Never doubt in your life
That JESUS will come any moment.

The doubt that you have, leave it in oblivion
The sign of miracles have been witnessed
The seeing of the blind, the walking of the
lame, the cure of the illness
All of these and many more will sweep the
dust of your doubts.

Even the power of casting evil, you can perform
Just say, "In the Name of JESUS," I cast you demon
Never doubt that it will go away and will be gone
Never doubt, the power of GOD is in your heart.

Change your doubt to devotion and ask GOD
for this grace
You will be given faith and belief and obedience
at the end
Yield to the Holy Spirit and see it for yourself
So never doubt, never doubt, the power of GOD
and the power of love.

THE HEART

They say that the size of the fist is the size
the heart,
The blood that runs through is the blood
of your life
The arteries, the veins, the coronaries and the small
muscles are part of the heart that make it pumps.
The heart is an important part of the body.
that gives sign that you are still alive fully.
When the heart is hurt and damaged
the joy and happiness disappeared
The heart can break, but can connect, patch and
can reconcile
The heart plays an important role in any relationship
You can speak from the mind and be boastful
But speaking from the heart is sweet and gentle
Sincerity it shows, and the heart can tell,
Heart conversation is the best of all.
The definition of love roots from the heart
It can describe and interpret a whole lot
The feeling you have, the emotion that triggers
the mind cooperates in expressing oneself
In the middle of any decision, heart and mind matters
That's why we need GOD's guidance in our discernment.
GOD speaks from His heart and His powerful mind.
Let's use our hearts to do His will and His commands.
In the Old Testament, GOD talked to one of the prophets
He said He would change their stony hearts to new ones.
He did it and the fulfillment is in the New Testament
He cleansed and created in them their new hearts.
O LORD, we thank You for changing our hearts
transforming our lives creating new ones.
So, allow us to use our hearts and not our minds
to work divinely here on earth towards Your Kingdom.

THE BOOK OF LIFE

Everyone in this world has a book of life to write,
has a book of life to read and has a book of life to share.
Every story has its origin, may it be dull or interesting,
so start looking at yourself and start writing about your
wonderful life the LORD GOD Has given.

> Have you ever asked your parents
> how you were when you were little?
> Have you ever felt the need to be
> recognized when you were growing?
> Have you ever been aware at all,
> of your surroundings?
> If you have wondered what life
> must have been,
> then, start journaling about yourself
> from the beginning.
> (The book of life I must say).
>
> Every page of your life has a meaning
> Every breath you take is essential
> Every move you make has a value
> For GOD Has a great plan for you.
> GOD loves to read our book of life
> For He is proud we're created
> in His Image
> He guides us in every move we make
> He is there every flip of the page
> He is the author of our life
> And we must respect that wonderful gift
> For we only live once in this lifetime
> So may GOD bless us and keep our
> Book of life in His heart . . . Choose life!

GREAT MOMENTS

What are the great moments in your life?
Stories after stories tell about
> the romance
> the success
> the accomplishment
> the healing
> the marriage
> and many more.

A mother is delight having a new
born baby in her arms.
A father just got a high paying job.
A child receives A's in his grades.
An orphan just adopted by a nice couple.
A patient goes home fully recovered.
An evicted person found a shelter.
Are these the great moments in your life?
Somebody does a random act of kindness,
a great moment for the recipient
Knowing our LORD from my heart
is one great moment
Having a deep relationship with JESUS
is my great moment
Feeling the warmth of our Blessed Mother,
my great moment
The power of the Holy Spirit is within me
my great moment
Telling others about how awesome our GOD
Is, my great moment
Having fellowship with my family and
and friends, my great moment
And most of all, the promise of salvation,
the promise of GOD to welcome me in
His Kingdom, the greatest moment.

My dear Readers,
Let us pray for our loved ones, who had gone ahead of us.
May eternal rest grant unto all the departed souls, O LORD.
Let perpetual light shine upon them. May they rest in peace.
Heavenly Father, please grant them Your mercy. Amen!

REMEMBERING YOU

Have you uttered these words to your loved ones?
"Moments to remember, time spent, lingering on
the thoughts of our togetherness . . ."
Yes, I whisper these in my heart every chance I have.
In my heart you have a special place
In my mind there are good memories to ponder
Remembering you is my only precious moment.

Remembering our loved ones is reminding us
that there'll be time that someone would be
thinking of us when we're gone.
Let us allow ourselves to reflect on how it is
to have a wonderful life,
a life full of blessings and graces from GOD.

Think of the time when your parent's words
were the only sounds you would like to hear.
Think of the giggles and laughs of your little ones
Think of the members of the family that you
wanted to hug, but not there anymore.
Then, realizing they are only in your memory lane.

Life is too short, like a treasure, life is temporary
Life is given to us to witness its essence and beauty
The essence of life when GOD created us in His
Image, and its beauty is when He welcomes us in
His kingdom.
The utmost and greatest gift we have is GOD's
Presence in our hearts, saying,
"Remembering you is my delight."

A TIME TO HEAL

A time to heal is a time to accept the truth
A time to heal is a time to ease the pain
A time to heal is a time to forgive
A time to heal is a time to be forgiven.

Healing is a process of cleansing
Healing is a transforming process
Healing is a gift from the Holy Spirit
And healing is a peace offering.

Healing leads to a reconciliation
Healing results from mortification
Healing makes us stronger ever
And healing nourishes our soul

We need to pray fervently
We need to meditate profoundly
We need to spend time with our LORD
And commune with Him in His Sanctuary
We need quality moments to ponder
And we need a time to heal for the
Awaited tranquility.

MOMENTS OF AWARENESS

We are always in a busy zone
We don't have time of our own
We don't even take time
To have moments of awareness.

When weekdays come, we start to rush
On weekends we have chores to finish
Where is our time to focus
On the moments of awareness.

The moments of awareness are
The moments of GOD's constant Presence
The moments of awareness are the moments
to ponder on Him
The moments of awareness are the moments
of acknowledging His deeds.
Yes, the moments of awareness should
be in our hearts.

Are we aware that JESUS is in
everyone's face?
Are we aware that the Holy Eucharist
is the Body of CHRIST?
Now, do we have awareness of Who GOD is?

The love that GOD has taught us
Is the love of each other's awareness
The awareness of one another and love for
GOD is the greatest of all.
The moments of awareness will lead us to
know GOD more
So, are we going to be aware of everyone's
presence and GOD's existence?

MY STRUGGLING HEART

My heart speaks out of gripes and pains
My heart craves for consoling words
My heart strives for an utmost peace
Yes, I do have a struggling heart.

I ask GOD to see my heart
I beg Him to feel my pain
I seek for His mercy and love
I want Him to touch my struggling heart.

LORD, this I beg for You to give
    fill my heart with Your wisdom
    fill my heart with humility
    fill my heart with Your love and mercy
    fill my heart with serenity
    fill my heart with understanding
    fill my heart with forgiveness
    fill my heart with inner healing
    fill my heart with peace
Yes my LORD fill me, my whole being
With holiness and worthiness
Fill my heart with tranquility, which
My heart longs to receive and this
Heart is Yours to keep.

FOOTPRINTS IN MY HEART

I know the story of "Footprints In The Sand,"
I know the message of its doubtfulness
I know GOD's reassurance of His care
But I didn't know that His footprints can
be in my heart.

When we walk in the sand, the footprints
are marked
But when someone else walked the same path
the footprints would be tampered
But in my heart GOD's footprints are engraved.

I feel the Presence of our LORD all the time
His voice is clear and it lingers in my ear
the message He gives, penetrates my being
Yes, His love marks as footprints in my heart.

When the sand is soaked by the sea waves
the footprints disappeared and totally vanished
But when I hear GOD's Word of love
it stays strong and permanently in my heart.

GOD's footprints in my heart is my guide
His footprints are not only to walk in the sand
but to talk to my heart, telling me, "that in my
heart He carries my whole being and my soul,"
Now, do you know whose footprints are in
your heart?

RETREAT OF SILENCE

I came to be with You my LORD in the
Sanctuary of Your heart
I came to talk to You in the silence
I came to listen to Your voice so soft
Here I am LORD in the Retreat Of Silence.

LORD, in here I started to reflect
I reflect on my old and existing sins
I searched for my lost soul indeed
And I seek for Your utmost forgiveness.

Now that I am away from the city
Away from the noise and turmoil
I now have time to be alone with You
to pour out myself, my pain and sorrow.

In my heart there is heaviness
In my mind there is confusion
In this place I found myself and
found You my LORD.
Yes my LORD, I am grateful to say
that I made the right discernment
to be with You in this Retreat Of Silence
I know that in Your time, time heals
And I feel You all the time, Your Presence.

Thank You my Father for embracing me
Thank You, my mother, the Blessed One,
for interceding
Thank You for allowing me to be reconciled
with You again
But most of all, thank You for I am
again forgiven
In Your name, I say and pray, Amen!

THE LONGEST TELEGRAM

Have you received a telegram lately?
If you haven't, don't be in a hurry
I have a telegram for you
And you will love it really.

It says, "GOD loves you unconditionally."
He is glad to do it without feeling sorry.
So please read more of this telegram
It's worth reading than any story.

You see that beautiful babe in the stable?
That's my Son when He was a Baby
He was smiling at you innocently
not knowing His future is to save the
world, so weary.

His humble parents named Joseph and
Mary, His only clan
Were there to support my wonderful plan
My plan to save the whole mankind
and to let you know they are forgiven.

When my Son was in His youth, people
admired Him.
He mingled with the elders with good intentions
He started to preach with strong conviction
And that was the beginning of His mission.

Then the time came and He was in His thirties
He picked ordinary trusted people
Fishermen, farmers and a tax collector
They were then called, "the twelve apostles."

The teaching, preaching and healing started
Until some envious groups viciously interfered
My Son's reputation was bruised and damaged.
That was the beginning of betrayal,
condemnation and hatred.

My Son's life was at stake
My plan for Him He humbly accepted
He was indeed sad and broken-hearted
And He was depressed, yet submissive.

Let me tell you my children, how He suffered
His flesh was torn, with His blood
continuously flowing
His mind was exhausted, the crown
on His head penetrated His scalp
a good half-inch
The nails on His Hands and Feet
were excruciating
But His soul was untouched, strongly
convicted to the commitment of the
promise of salvation.
My children, let me pause for a moment
to give you time to exhale
I want you to respond to this longest telegram
with the hope that you will ponder and reflect
the time You started to know our LORD JESUS
and the moment you realized you are saved.

I hope to hear from you soon, my child.
I signed as Your Maker and Savior forever.

THE AMAZING BOOK

The greatest story ever told is in the Bible
The Bible is the best seller in the whole world
It tells the story of mankind and creation
and the origin of our parents and its generation
The prophets in the Bible are the anointed people
they live in holiness and have been transformed
from the prophets in the Old Testament to the
disciples of the New Testament
They have something in common, they were
followers of the LORD's Son JESUS.
The Bible is a book of reference, a book of
virtue and a book of knowledge
It is a guidance for everything and anything
that you can imagine
The proverbs, the psalms, the canticles of the
prophets are just overwhelming and worth reading.
You can tell a story to your small kids from the Bible
They will have fun and will have knowledge
They will know at young age who their original
parents were;
They will find out how the earth was created
For the adulthood, the Bible is recommended
They will have wonderful virtues to follow
They can start their lives in a righteous way
They will be model parents for their own children
There are mysterious things that the Bible offer
If you're weary, tired, worried and troubled
There are pages in the Bible for the answers

Your troubles then will be shifted to triumphs.
Another thing you can attain when you
read the Bible is the wisdom that is freely
given and can be passed on.
It's up to you to avail, accept and use it
So it is not too late yet fellow readers
Start opening your Bible, read it diligently
Ponder from your heart, have a reflective mind
And don't let your Bible stay on the shelf
To accumulate dust.

THE BIBLE IS YOUR LIFE
YOUR LIFE IS BIBLICAL

TRANSFORMATION

"I was once lost and blind, but now I see,"
A popular line in a beautiful song,
"Amazing Grace," is the song title
It lingers in our mind for so long.

Our yesteryears were full of trials and successes
Engrossed with fame and riches
No time for GOD, to even say thanks
Full of greed and discontentment.

You adore the luxury, the money and the power
You didn't even know what to do and where to go
With this bunch of treasures in the locker
spending lavishly without control.

No time to reflect, to ponder on the source
of your wealth
You brag that you are not only good, but the best
And one day you felt sad so suddenly
You felt uncertain, confused, depersonalized,
Not knowing it is calling.

You cried so hard, called GOD and asked,
"Why LORD, I felt lost and confused?"
"I don't know what to do and where to go and
whom to talk?"
"LORD, will you help me in this dungeon?"

The dungeon that was mentioned, is just an analogy
And it only describes the depth of anxiety
The panic attack that the person is experiencing
is not punishment, but a blessing.

When GOD calls someone, it comes in different ways
It could be a tragedy, failure, tribulation or illness
Or it could be in the middle of searching Him
Wherever, whatever and however it is, He'll
meet you crossways.

Now, you'll start knowing who JESUS CHRIST is
and realized GOD's love
You went through your sins' repentance to be a
Christian, and you start loving yourself and the
people around, and you know now to love GOD
with all your heart, mind, strength and soul.

You have changed a lot, your characters and goals
You are now faithful with your daily prayer time
You serve the LORD through the community
and church
You are now a renewed person and went through
Holy transformation.

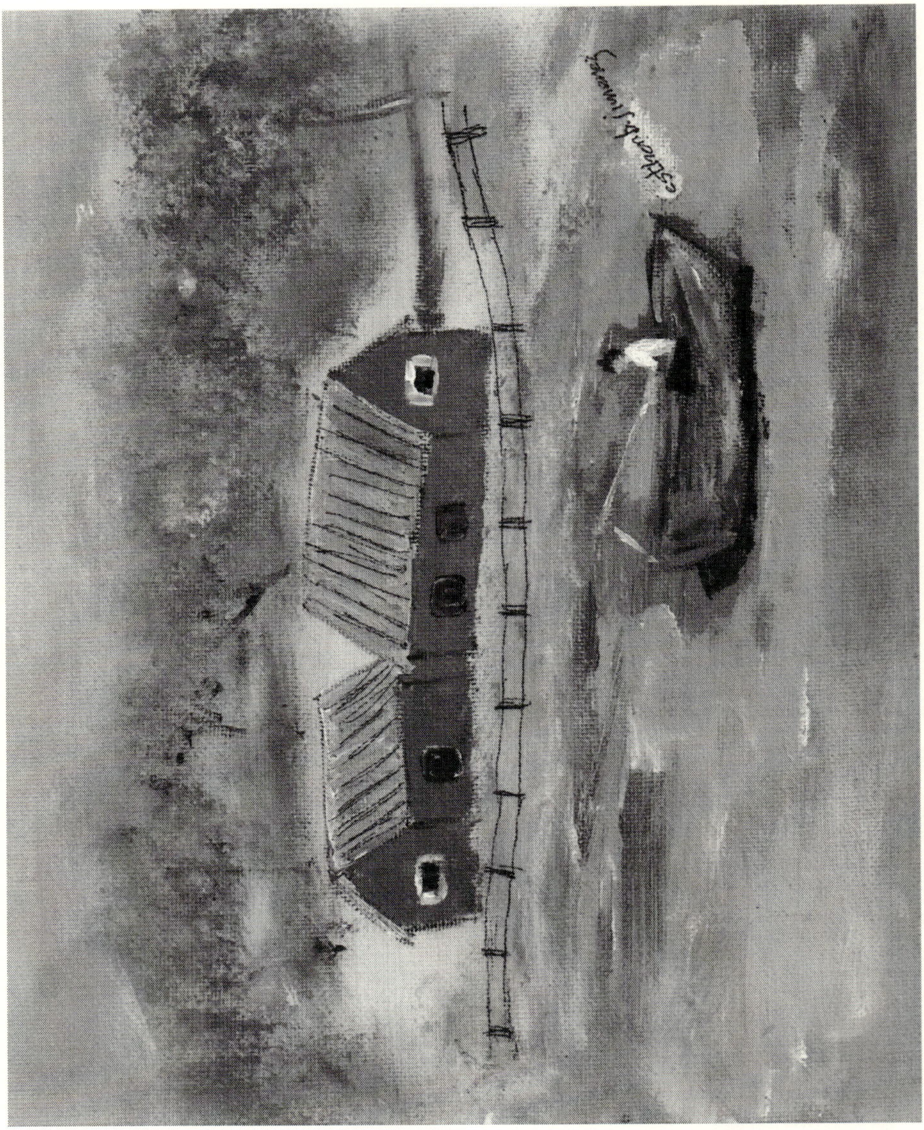

CHAPTER II

A POEM FOR EVERYONE
AND
ABOUT SOMEONE

How would you like to read something about you and your name, describing your good quality traits? This chapter is all about knowing the people around you through what they do and what they accomplish in this world. I love to write acronyms, especially the names of people I know and the people I encounter. I described them according to their traits. Lately, I started writing poems about people (their profession, vocation, requested poems like for pets, friends, relatives, etc.) A poem for everyone is about you, about me, and about them. I have a separate chapter for the acronyms and sub-chapter for the homonyms. They'll be in the last few pages.

NOTE: One time, I handed a copy of the poem about "The Mailmen," to our mailman and he showed it to his co-workers. They decided to post it in their bulletin board, for them to see it everyday. You can do the same, if you find something about you and your profession, you can cut it, you can even laminate it, (provided they are not copyrighted), or you can ask permission from the author. How about giving a corresponding poem to your friends or relatives for who they are?

A POEM FOR EVERYONE

Whoever You Are, Whatever You Do,
I Can Write Something Related To You,
Just Let Me Know, Call Me Or Do Write,
I'll Create A Poem That Will Fit You Alright.
The Phone Number Is 361-2246 Area Code 630
The Address Is Somewhere in Illinois, known as
the Windy City and here is a poem for you, a poem
for me and a poem for everybody

OUR LADY

There are many prayers and novenas for our Mother
All of them are powerful intercessions
We ask, we beg and meditate on her virtues,
Our Lady thank you for interceding.

We honor and respect you, our Mother
You are our model of perfection
You are a Blessed Virgin and a true martyr
Our Lady help us in our transformation.

You have appeared in different countries
You give messages to the chosen ones
You urge people to say the rosary
You really take care of our souls profoundly.

We clasp our hands and bow down to you
to show our profound reverence
We are glad to have you as our Mother
And the Mother of our Savior.

You have done a lot of miracles and healing
You are given different honorary respective names
to signify the miracles happened in different places
Each time of the apparition, you are always in action.

We go to places of your apparition
We say the litanies on those occasions
We give you honor on every first Saturdays
Our Lady thank you for your love, mercy and care.

Dear Lady, our Blessed Virgin Mary
You are awesome like your Son
You lamented to the redemptive suffering
You witnessed, your Son's hurtful groaning.

When we say the Hail Mary not once, but many
We know the consequence and the indulgence
And when we ponder on the Canticle of Mary
Our souls rejoice with the LORD Almighty.

The song, "Magnificat" is a powerful inspiration
We are reassured of GOD's protection
We are secured with the cover of your mantle
We are loved by our Lady, who is so wonderful.

Your virtues are commendable and admirable
You taught us to be obedient and humble
We can have these through your intercession
Our Lady we ask you to continue guarding our souls.

I wrote this on September 02, 2000, Our Lady's Day, first Sunday of September.

OUR MOTHER, THE BLESSED

How awesome just to know you're there
How peaceful my mind is, feeling your warmth
How great the Holy Spirit, generous with His gifts
The gift I received, the love of our Mother,
the Blessed
Our Mother, thank you for aiding me in
my daily life
For interceding in my every strife;
The love and care that you extend
The help we need, you do can sense.
Our Mother, can I call you my mother?
"Yes, my dear child", your holy answer
I feel secured now and in every moment
because I know what my heart says,
"You are loved by your mother, isn't it great?
When I pray the "Hail Mary," the fullness
of your grace I feel,
The assurance that the LORD is with Thee
My weapon in this world I see
You bless among the rest of the world
the women you behold, the fruit that you
bear, the Savior of us all.
O my Holy Mother of GOD, thank you
for praying for us, not only for our needs
but for our great sins
You love us now and even to the time
of our last moments.
I love you my dear Mother and bless us
now and forever. Amen!

TO OUR BLESSED MOTHER, I CRY

Awesome, this Beloved Mother
Gentle heart she has
Warm embrace she is willing to extend
Our Blessed Mother always intercedes.

Humble Lady, full of mercy
Great intercessor, full of grace
We love you so dearly, our Mother
to you, the Blessed I pray fervently.

My Mother, my confidant
You help me in my plea
You ask your Son to listen to me
As obedient as you are, He adores
You truly
Yes, I cry to you my Mother Mary.

Mary Immaculate, our Lady of
Assumption, you deserve the beautiful
names given to you.
You appeared to many places, with messages
O Mary, my Mother I cry to you
and honor you so dearly.

I pray O Mary for your intercession
To have peace in this world
To say the rosary as often as we can
To have a total conversion of mankind
Yes, to you my Blessed Mother, I cry
for your love and mercy
I pray in your Son's name forever, Amen!

OUR FATHER—THE POPE

We salute you Pope John Paul II
For your love and care to mankind
For being a model of holy tenacity
And for your spiritual hospitality
People love you (regardless of race)
They honor you with profound reverence
You are a true disciple of GOD
A faithful successor of St. Peter
You are intelligent and full of wisdom
You love to share your holiness
You are so involved with world issues
And you take care of our souls
You write many inspirational books
You visit a lot of places around
You give spiritual talks so powerful
To the youth, they are respectful
Your spiritual strength is admirable
You are an inspiration and so wonderful
Your Holiness, our father is commendable
We pray for you and your health fervently
We pray for more blessings from the Almighty.
We love You Holy Father, our Pope forever.

MOTHER ANGELICA

I honor you mother for your brave heart
I learn a lot from your sharing
I love to hear you laugh
And I ponder on your teachings.
The viewers enjoy your program
They look forward for the good news
The Good News that you always taught
From the Bible, the genuine source.
EWTN is one of my favorites
It gives me joy and delight
Because of you, Mother Angelica
The network is now at large.
I've been praying for you ever since
For your health and peace as well
For your spiritual tenacity
And for your longevity.
I love you Mother and I bless you
I will continue to watch you
I will ask GOD for more graces
for you Mother and all your concerns
May GOD Bless you and your work,
And may the Holy Spirit guide you
every step of the way.
May our Blessed Mother intercede with us
and for us, I pray this in JESUS name, Amen!

BLESSED ARE THE HANDICAPS

Let's pause for a moment and ponder
on the thoughts of how lucky we are
to have a thought process.
Now, let's imagine a person who can't see,
blind totally, those who can't speak and
can't talk, or those with difficulty of speech.
How about the deaf, who can't hear, and
those who can't walk, or no limbs at all
And yet, there are those who can hear, can
talk, can see and walk, but no insights at all.
Their insights were stolen by severe
depression, drugs, narcotics and alcohol,
mentally handicaps are the mentally
retarded (what they call mentally challenge)
and mentally-ill.
So, aren't we lucky we can hear, talk, see
and walk?
Not so! Not so! Not so!
For there are some people who can do
anything and everything, but they lack the
essence of compassion.
So let's be content, with what we have
We are lucky, but handicaps are blessed.
They are our mentors in our spirituality.
GOD loves them and blesses them all.
We are handicaps too in some points
But we are recipients of GOD's graces
So cheers to all, including the handicaps,
Let's rejoice for we are all created in
GOD'S IMAGE.

GOLDEN MOMENTS

Golden Moments, a nice title for a poem
very appropriate for the stage of my life now
And to be a half century age is an accomplishment.
You only age by years and not in heart.
Life starts at fifty, I may say
and it is the climax of the century
You get the chance to be in the golden
years' award
You reach the precious moments of your life.
You can be young parents or grandparents
Dignity and honor you're proud to have,
Standing firm in front of the crowd
Yes, golden moments, golden times shared,
let's treasure them
Life is too short, let's not make it shorter
Enjoy your golden moments and share your graces
Let us thank our Almighty for every year that
He adds in our lives
Let us appreciate every moment of that gift
Let us give honor to the seniors in our own
family and in the home facility
But most of all, let us honor our GOD for
our golden moments
Cheers to all the years, cheers to the coming
years, I praise our Almighty for everything!

SENIOR MOMENTS

The leaves are falling
The twigs are brittle
The trunk is shaky
Are we talking about a tree?

They claim they know you
They think you are related
They grasp things momentarily
Are we really their relatives?

No, we are not talking about a tree
No, we are not their relatives
But yes, they are created in
GOD's Image
Yes these are the elder people
With senior moments.

Sweet and gentle, these people are
They stare blankly and talk
irrelevantly
Honor and respect, they do deserve
These are the beautiful people
with senior moments
Shall we remember them,
in our moments of awareness?

LOVE AT FIRST SIGHT

I have a short story to tell
It's about a young lady who
is pregnant at teen;
She always touches her belly
and feels the movement within;
In her abdomen is where the
heart is, of that beautiful being.
On the ninth month, the mother
feels the frequency of the
movement of the baby wanting
to come out.
Alas! The long awaited has now
come, another miracle of life!
The tears, the smile and the sweat
are the signs of her love at first sight,
seeing this fragile infant.
The question asks is, "How can
you love someone you
just met?"
The answer is, "GOD's love is
where the heart is."
That's the end of my story, and I
dedicate this to all young mothers
who are blessed with the gift of
life within her life.

A MESSAGE OF THE UNBORN

"I am a few days old mommy
going to be few weeks, then months
I ask you please to be patient
for a few months more is worthy to wait.
Whatever the cause of my existence
it is your will to choose
to be with me when I come out
to enjoy the gift of life.
I understand you're only human
So, ask the grace of GOD
Listen to the prompt of the Holy Spirit
He'll grant you the peace of mind
The gift that you'll receive
is not only the gift of discernment
but the gift that you'll treasure
forever in your heart
It's me mommy your adorable baby
coming soon on this earth
I love you mommy."

TODDLERS—TOTS

Terrible "2", terrible "3",
toddlers they are called
with motile behavior
always saying no.
Another favorite word
they utter is, "It's mine"
"It's mine", and they don't
want to hear, "It's a no—no."
These tots are incredible
They are cute, lovable and
adorable.
I don't have kids, I have
nephews and nieces
I love them all.
They are my treasures,
for me they are so precious;
Toddlers walk the same
wobbling, and waggling like ducklings
They are clumsy for one thing
Multiple slips and falls happen,
but whatever I say
Toddlers-tots you are amazing
You're angels in our eyes
Most of all, you are the angels
in GOD's sight.

THANK YOU AMERICA

I can't help but shed my tears today
Thanksgiving Day, when I heard the
song, "America, The Beautiful."
An immigrant like me is very grateful
for the chance that GOD Has given me,
to live in a place like the United States.

An overwhelming feeling that I felt
standing on the pew of the church,
singing aloud this beautiful song
Yes, America is beautiful, with the
opportunities given to people
regardless of race, I salute your flag
as my profound reverence.

The land of liberty, the land we migrated
that is none other than the United States
The help that we extend to our families afar,
the benefits we receive here and there
I am most grateful for this country so rare
I thank GOD for everything, including
the blessing of this country we live in,
America, the beautiful.
Thank You our Almighty, thank you America!

We were on our way to Ohio and I was enjoying the scenery, especially the cornfields, rice fields and other crops. Then I thought of acknowledging the farmers for their industriousness and tenacity in taking care of the fields.

THE FARMER AND THE FIELDS

A wide land at the side of the road
Full of green and brownish stalks
Cornfields and rice fields in the farm
ready for harvest any moment.

The seeds that the farmers planted
The soils that they tilled
The crops that they harvested
came from the land called, fields.".

We eat everyday, we shop for food
We see greens, crops and other produce
Recognition we seldom do
for these farmers in the fields, hitherto.

The different crops that the farmers harvest
Are distributed around and picked the best
Fruits and vegetables and fresh tomatoes
Are all the products of the farmers' effort

Let us give thanks to GOD for the fields
and the farmers,
That brought His abundance on earth
And on Thanksgiving Day, let us not forget
To acknowledge the farmers and the fields.

I was working at the nursing home with some women employed who were at prison rehab. They were going back to the rehab place every after eight hour work. I had the chance to listen and find out the story why they were imprisoned. I was glad then, that they were given a chance to be out and made their living. This poem is for them and all women in prison.

THE REFORMED

They spent time in a prison cell
They paid their dues, must we tell?
They made mistakes, in the dungeon
they fell
For some of them, prison is a hell.
Everyday they look forward to be out.
"Hope" is what they keep them alive
"Living one day at a time", becomes
their motto,
To live their lives to the fullest, to look
for tomorrow.
I dedicate this poem, to all the people
in prison
And especially for the women, a mother,
a wife, a divorcee, and a single one,
for their courageous hearts, tenacity
and patience;
For their humility, faith and obedience.
At last, the reward came into their lives,
"Freedom", finally from the secluded place
"The Reformed," as they are called, molded
to transform
They are beautiful people, in GOD's Image,
they are created.
GOD Bless all the reformed and all the
people in the prison.

THE JURORS

Twelve people mixed with male and female
Black, White, Hispanic, Asian, anyone?
Who could be a juror?
People gathered in the court room,
not allowed to discuss the case with each
other at all, behind the court house.
They argue, they agree, they come in unity
One or two may say "nay", it'll be a mistrial;
The verdict is in the hands of the twelve,
A thorough analysis is needed,
No one really knows, if the accused is
guilty or not, but there is Only One Who
Knows The Truth, and it is our LORD GOD.
So, if you're one of the jurors
please ask GOD for the gift of discernment
Let us offer our prayers for every accused
and victims, that they may have justice and
peace whatever the consequence is.

THE MAILMEN

Mailmen are angels on this earth
They deliver letters, sort of messages
They walk from house to house
from block to block, just to connect
between people in our lives.
Rain or shine, snow or flood
they are on the streets with their mail bags
They drive cars, stirring wheel on the right
to facilitate their job on the street side.
Just imagine, the feeling of waiting
for the letters in the making
excited and happy to receive
a love letter, a package, anything
that is expected to be in ones hand.
We should be thankful for the mailmen
and mailwomen for taking care of our
postal needs and packages, accommodating
in the office, showing their expertise on
on how our mails are to be protected.
Let us salute these people in light
blue-grayish uniform that are devoted
to their job and serving us all.
May our LORD continue to bless them
and their families,
Thank You GOD, for creating angels
on earth, "the mailmen", the "mailwomen"

THE FIREMEN

One of the heroes in this world
Are men wearing red hats and
yellow coats
Holding huge hose attached to
a hydrant
Sprinkling water to the blazing fire.

Back draft is what they always face
Saving lives they always aim
Firemen they are, noble people
A professional job, always in motion.

I salute the firemen all over the world
For their brave hearts and strength
For their quick thinking and fast moves
For the love to serve mankind.

When you hear a loud siren and see
a red truck
Drive aside or stop, or they would be stuck
The hydrant in front of the building or house
is a life saver that saves many lives.

Not only they are trained in hosing the fire
They are also trained to do the CPR
So let us include the firemen in our prayers
and their families, and bless them always.

THE SECRETARIES

You are in the front line
giving an impression
to the people that come
in unexpected invitation
Without you, the phone is dead
A ghost ring of the telephone
No human touch
But with your "hello" and
a great smile
It's pleasing and warm to the
receiver on the other line
"Secretary", you are called
a good nature I must conclude
a Day like this shouldn't
be forgotten
A special Day for the secretaries,
You deserved to be honored.

Happy Secretaries Day!

THE CRAFTERS

We do our stuff from scratch
We assemble little things at large
We take time to do our projects
We are humbly called, "The Crafters"
We look forward to the weekend's
art and craft show
Even on weekdays we don't fail to go
We have our shows at school gym or
basement
We have them on the side of the streets
with canopy and tent
We meet different people and gain
new friends
Crafters we are, artists as well
We are here to share the wonder
of wonders
The gifts that we received from
our Creator.

SPECIAL PEOPLE

(In Reading Poetry)

We are the poets around the corner
We are not celebrities
But we are the expressionists
And we speak from the heart
Of the things we want.

I listen to the reading of their poems
In my heart, I am amazed and thrilled
The talents that the poets showed
are the wonderful experience they have
encountered.

The feelings they have, expressed in poems
The wisdom they attained are generously
shared.
The youth, the adult, the women and
the men are here tonight.
Reading, sharing, their work of art, spoken
from the heart.
I am glad, I'm with them, the special people.

A SMILE

Have you ever heard the sound of a smile?
It is pleasing and warm even at a distant mile
It is soothing and therapeutic to see a smiling face
It is uplifting, couple with hug and embrace.

A smile every moment is an every moment joy
In the hearts of the receiver it's a precious toy
A smile creates a new friendship
And turn friendship to a gentle relationship.

Smile takes less percent of facial muscle
Frown takes more and it's a hassle
So, try to smile often and be genuine
You change the world this way, it's a challenge.

There's a line from a song that says,
"Smile, though your heart is aching,"
Is indeed true, "even though it's breaking,"
And because, GOD is always there,
To take care of our inner healing,
Smile! And the world would smile at you,
Is a great feeling!

THE RETIREES

A long service in the job,
Can't wait to relax
Loyalty, I should say,
Brings reward at last
These people are called
"the retirees," I salute them
for their endurance, patience
and for working hard.

They battled with the labor
fought for their rights
They stayed in unity with
their common goals,
They are sometimes not recognized
But now they are retirees,
And they deserve it.

Now that they are not working
as regular employees
They are working for themselves
And they plan for a spree
A lot of time and space awaits for them
to enjoy their moments of being free.
Congratulations! "the retirees,"
Especially to our favorite friend,
"Rick," at last a retiree."
Enjoy your long awaited moments
of relaxation.

THE HOUSEKEEPING

How can you keep the house
if you don't own it?
How can we ever know the
essence of housekeeping
if you don't pay attention to
what it is?
A house that is not clean
is not a home to live in
Housekeeping is important in
maintaining a home
Whether you have your family
or you're alone
Not only in houses that
housekeeping is needed,
we need to have a clean
surrounding
In the hospitals and any
community living,
housekeeping is a noble job
Without the housekeepers a
place is a dust slab
So, let us respect the people
in this department
or the environment
Remember, cleanliness is next
to Godliness.

THE CARPENTERS

You live in a beautiful house
You admire the way it's been built
You know it's done from scratch
The carpenters are the ones to
be recognized

Builders are around the world
And carpenters are one of them
They are skilled in building, buildings
houses after houses, condos after condos.

Life can be compared to building a house
In which GOD is the Master Builder
But He Has a Worker Who is an expert
His Son CHRIST JESUS,
the Greatest Carpenter

So let us acknowledge all the carpenters
Who did our houses and put them together
And let's also live our lives to the fullest
Because our Master Builder is Perfect
And the Best!

A TEACHER

It starts with the alphabets and numbers
It starts at pre-school age utmost
It is the beginning of a grand lesson
by the teacher in a classroom.
A teacher and a mother trade-in places
A teacher as second mother, a mother
as second teacher
With the support of this model image
A successful student becomes a sage.
A teacher is an expert for beginners
She works hard, and with her is her daily
lesson plans
She is patient, articulate and creative
She is someone to be recognized
at any chance moment.
Teaching is essential part of our lives
We learn to live our lives to the fullest
We learn not only the ABC and the 123,
We learn the essence of each word and
life's accountability.
But one thing we should know about
a certain Teacher,
He teaches every human to be divine
He commands us to love one another
He always Has Good News to tell
And that Teacher is none other than
CHRIST JESUS,
The Doeth and all knowing LORD
So let us acknowledge all teachers
And salute them for their accomplishments
They are the pioneers of initial lessons
They are special people truly GOD's creations.

CAREGIVER

I wake up in the morning to prepare things for you
I make your breakfast and feed you if I need to
I give you your morning care from your hair to your toe
I fix your bed smooth and clean, I am a caregiver.

I watch you all day long and all night through
I assist you in daily living and in all your moves
I keep quiet and I respect your bad moods
I cheer with you in good spirit, I am caregiver.

I walk with you enjoying the breeze
I sympathize with you in your low moments
I listen to your sighs and share with you my shoulder
I care about you, I am a caregiver.

I read you stories and I sing with you.
I ran errand for extra things that you need
I pray in silence for your recovery and peace
I am here for you, I am a caregiver.

A caregiver that I am, needs someone too
To care for me, my soul and my being
I know that GOD is my hope and strength
He cares for me, He is the best Caregiver.

LORD, I thank you for creating the caregivers
Who care for a weak and physically disabled
Give them more strength, LORD, spiritually
So they can minister more in the community
Caregiver, I am called, here I am at your service.

THE DOCTOR

What are we going to do without
doctors in this world, who take care
of our pains and complaints, who
prescribe medicines, order x-ray
and laboratory exam, who take
vital signs and do physical exams?
A physician, another name for a
doctor, has long good years of
education, must be diligent, must
have compassion, perseverance and
tenacity and must be conscientious.
One very sure about doctors, they
were given to us by our Creator.
It is even in the Bible about why
GOD created doctors, that is to
serve the needy and ill mankind.

As I described the nurse in this poem, I am thinking of typical Filipino nurses who struggle to pursue their nursing career.
As one Filipino culture, parents make sure that their children have better education, they strive for that betterment. I am relating how nurses attained their nursing education, the rests are my description of who nurses are, (Filipino or non-Filipino).

A NURSE

She went to school to study, to be like Florence Nightingale
Florence Nightingale was the very first nurse in ancient history
During internship, a nurse learned the tender, loving, care
the kind of care needed by the clients.
After graduation, this nurse looks for a job
she works in the hospital with flexible shift.
A nurse is a well-rounded person
Takes care of a client's whole being
Gives morning and evening care including giving medication.
She tries to finish her tasks within eight hours, carries doctor's orders diligently, and coordinates with other members of the staff.
There are three H's that are significant about nurses. A nurse uses her *head,* for decision, discernment and discretion.
Her *hand,* in rendering bedside care, giving medication,
Her *heart* she uses with compassion
I salute the nurse for their H's.
I salute all nurses including my relatives,
I thank our Almighty for creating the nurses.

This was my eulogy for Josie. May you rest in peace, and let the perpetual light shine upon you.

THAT'S HER JOSIE

Wonderful lady, beautiful woman,
That's her Josie
Kind hearted person, good mother to
Kiel and Kenyon
A caring grandma to Dominick
(the one and only one)
That's her Josie
A compassionate nurse, a loyal friend
A generous lady
And an obedient daughter, an understanding
sister, that's her Josie
An industrious housewife, a loving one
a Jack of all trades, an artist, a chef,
Mind you, I am proud of her,
That's her Josie.
She crocheted unique center pieces
She liked to read amazing passages
There was always beauty in her
in heart and in deeds
Again, who was she? That's her Josie.
Josie, my sister in CHRIST
You'll be missed a lot
You'll be remembered now and forever
Because you have planted beautiful seeds
in our hearts.
We loved you and we blessed you
May GOD be with you till eternity.

JOSIE will be busy crocheting center pieces with our initials on them and she will offer them to our Creator, in the center of His Heart!

THE CLOWN

I attended a children's party and there was a clown who was entertaining the kids. I've seen clown's performances many times, but I never paid attention, until this moment. Kids are really amused, So here is a poem for them and about them.

He makes the kids laugh, cheers the adult ones
He gives happiness to the crowds
He lets the doves come out from the handkerchief
He does magic trick of bunny on the hat.
He puts weird make-up on his face
His hair-do is blonde, red and Afro-like
He has a red rubbery bulb-size nose
He wears a pair of torn giant shoes
The clothes he wears are loose and garter-y
With huge bow tie on his neck
Designs of his clothes are polka dots and stripes
Looking at his attire, very colorful and contrast
He can play card tricks with unusual numbers
He can make balloons in different shapes
He can joggle bowling pins and anything round
He likes to involve the happy audience to participate
He is so talented with a lot of tricks
He is good in mimics and imitations
He can do a top dance and dance a waltz
He can play with different instruments through
His imagination
His guitar doesn't have strings
His piano doesn't make sounds
But he can create music from his heart
This beautiful person called himself, "Clown."

A clown is also created by GOD
with special role on this earth
To let the people know that life is like a clown
laughing in the outside, inside they cry
Thank you, Mr. Clown/ Miss Clown and the rest
of your gang
For entertaining us in our leisure time
May the power of GOD be with you and may
GOD continue to bless you,
Keep up the good work and we'll see
you next circus.

TO PONDER ON 911

It's not the place, it's not the people
It's not the fate, it's how the death occurs
It's not an illness, it's not a suicide
It's not just an ordinary accident;
It's the viciousness of the terrorists
It hurts, it lingers, it is unforgettable
Not only for the relatives of the victims
But even for a regular bystander
It won't be the same, it won't ever change
But we can continue to pray more fervently
for GOD's continuous love, mercy,
guidance and protection
And to help us from evil doers and their
satanic intentions
Most of all, for peace in our hearts forever!
LORD, I pray that You will guide us every
step of the way, especially the victim's
relatives and loved ones. Please help them
in their grieving process, in JESUS name,
I pray Amen!

THE PUNCH LINE

Laughter, they said is the best medicine
It's a therapy for feeling melancholic
Good thing we have comedians around
They can always share with us their
punch line.

When you're feeling down
And need a temporary relief
Go turn your television and search
for a channel
A channel that runs a comedy program.

Somebody has to do the entertaining
To make people laugh, for few moments
To forget the reality for a while
And join the crowds with the comedians.

Comedians are talented with special gift
Gift that is also given by GOD
Our LORD Has a sense of humor too
He knows whom to give the punch line clue.

So whenever you hear any punch line
From the comedians or your friends around
Remember that is not self-accomplishment
It is GOD who gave them the talents

There is a positive(+) and negative(-) humor
Choose the one with cross sign.

SHORTENING THE LIFE

We are on our way
to downtown Chicago
from our place in Itasca
a suburb of Illinois;
We saw an old lady
of about sixty
picking-up cigarette butts
from the sidewalk street
She has a short stick of
cigarette in her finger
and she lights every butt
she picks-up
She smokes continuously
lights the butts endlessly
Shortening her life, isn't she?
Through lengthening the
light, could it be?
LORD, please guide this old
precious lady whomever and
wherever she may be.

This is the presentation I did during our echo-conference. We were assigned to different sheep and we have to portray the kind of sheep we belong. Our group was assigned to a confused sheep. As performers, we could dance, role-play, sing, etc. But we decided that I should just read the poem that I wrote. And so I recited the poem, followed with another prayer poem. In the next page is the prayer I read and my sisters in CHRIST followed me and everyone was saying the prayer together.

THE POETRY OF THE CONFUSED SHEEP

We are the women who focus too much on ourselves
We think highly of the things we have accomplished
We take care of our own needs and not depend on others
Yes we are proud of ourselves being independent.

We are the leaders/ members of the community
We are engrossed with the task of service
We do have fun, friendship and fellowship
We feel great but at times we glorify ourselves.

The pride in our hearts poisons our minds
We put the attitude of humility aside
The Presence of the LORD are being ignored
And the leadership is being misused.

That's not the vision to focus on
That's not the mission to look forward to
That's not the ideal women of GOD
And that's not the kind of sheep to behold.

We belong to the flock of ninety-nine
Let's not be the sheep who went astray, got lost
Let's be the sheep with conviction to hold on
To the women of GOD's vision and mission.

What are we going to do, to be the deserving sheep?
What do we need to know to follow the Shepherd's steps?
How do we know we are one of GOD's flock?
Whom shall we call in the midst of the sheephold?

Let us open our contrite hearts
Let us use all the virtues we need
Let us ask for the grace to do GOD's will
Let us hold on to our Good Shepherd,
our LORD JESUS,
And let us serve Him with all our heart,
mind and soul.

We are no longer the struggling and
confused sheep
We are now the humble, focused sheep
with strong conviction
We are now the women of Good Shepherd.

Now that you've heard the poetry of the
confused sheep
Let me offer you a short prayer for the
Good Shepherd
When I say the prayer, please close your eyes
And ponder on the greatness of our
LORD JESUS, the Good Shepherd.

I do not want to lose our moments of pondering on our Good Shepherd, so I am including the Prayer next to this page. This prayer can also be found in Volume I of What's In My Heart?

PRAYER FOR THE GOOD SHEPHERD

O LORD our GOD, The Good Shepherd of our hearts, thank You so much for laying down Your life for us, Your humble servants.
We praise You LORD for leading us to the waters of peace, for Your watchful care to Your erring sheep. When we stumble and fall in this chaotic world, we ask You LORD to pasture us Your women of GOD's sheep hold. We beg You LORD to hear our voices through the streams, fields and every desert.
May You guide us O LORD to the right pathway, without any doubt and without any fear of evil; May You anoint us with Your love, mercy and care, and may the Holy Spirit empower us every step of the way, all this O LORD we pray through the intercession of Your Blessed Mother in Good Shepherd's name Our LORD JESUS, Amen!

I attended our class reunion of (1970, graduates of Marian School of Nursing) held in Los Angeles, California and it was at least thirty-two years ago. Since, it's human nature to be conscious of the physical aspect, the weights and hair losses, I thought of writing a poem about the real essence of a reunion. This is for my classmates and for anyone attending a reunion. As we speak of the year, it would be forty one years ago this year, (2011)

THE CLASS '70 REUNION

Few years have gone after graduation
Each has different plans and directions
Some stay in our country land
Some go abroad and further their plans
Exciting events, this Class'70 awaits
To see familiar faces with warm embrace
Some with family and some stay single
They look forward to be bonded again
So dear classmates of long ago
Let's enjoy the events together
Together let us show our compassion
It doesn't matter how we look like
It matters how we love and care
Thirty-two years is a lot of catching up
We can fill the space even for short moments
Class'70, Beautiful People, Congratulations,
For this Happy Reunion!

THE FELLOWSHIP

People are gathered, greeting each other
Hugging and shaking hands with smiles
Finding their seats whispering a little
Then everyone stood up to start the prayer.
The speaker is introduced with utmost respect
The topic of the talk is about "fellowship".
They listen to the speaker with joy seen in their faces
These are the group of young adults and seniors
After the talk they mingle, share and welcome
The unfamiliar faces
Coffee served, cookies and other goodies
But there is Someone watching them with a
Beautiful smile on His face
He is none other than our LORD JESUS,
greeting, nodding, shaking hands with the folks
and silently joining their fellowship.
Remember, JESUS is in the face of everyone!

This is a confession of a friend of mine, a lot younger than me, and she treats me as her mother. I added the word prayer in the title because this is my prayer for her. It should be in Volume I, but it is more appropriate to be in this chapter because this chapter is about a poem for everyone and about someone . .

A CONFESSION PRAYER.

O LORD, a friend of mine just called me
today, to pour out her ill-feelings
She's like a daughter to me, I started to listen
She confessed a delicate matter with
Slight feelings on her part, and she
felt like she is not worthy of Your love.
We were in tears while on the phone
So I asked the help of the Holy Triune
I thank You LORD for the enlightenment,
for letting us feel Your Presence
LORD we know You are a forgiving GOD
and You always extend Your healing power.
LORD JESUS, our Comforter, thank You
for mediating, for guiding us every step
of them way.
We pray this in JESUS name, Amen!

This is for a friend who is wanting so much to have peace in her heart. She expressed to me her sentiments about her best friend, her desire to be reconciled with her. This poem is a combination of her thoughts and desire and my wishes and prayer for their peace and reconciliation.

YOU'RE SO NEAR AND YET SO FAR

I drive everyday just to see your place
And many times I wanted to stop by,
just to say, "hello,"
But there's my fear of hearing the words,
"please go,"
So I just shook my head and wait for
another tomorrow.

Tomorrow might not come
Today I still have that plan of letting you
know my sincere intention
to offer my peace and be forgiven.

Life is too short and I can only do my best
My humble wish is to have a greater peace
I know the LORD is listening
In Him I lift up everything, including my
wish to be at peace with you, my friend.
May GOD bless us in our daily endeavor
May our reconciliation be at hand and soon
my friend, you're so near and yet so far.

A MEMORABLE WEEKEND

The clan from Illinois drove with the mini-van
to spend a weekend at Clarinda, Iowa as the plan
At dawn on Saturday, we left Orland Park
and reached Iowa in due time.

It was a heartwarming experience indeed
to hug and embrace the family you missed
The love and compassion that each shared
It was an overwhelming, unforgettable scene.

We thank You O LORD for the chance of a lifetime
To be reunited with families and friends
for the fellowship, bonding and precious moments
and for the healing that You have granted.

We know O LORD that it is only the beginning
of the wonderful sharing and bonding
There would be more time to share our
moments with them and with You
Thank You for the memorable weekend.

The Handmaids of the LORD is one of the ministries of CFC (Couples For CHRIST). H.O.L.D. is what they called handmaids for short and is composed of women who are single at least 40 years old with old, wives whose husbands are not ready yet to join, single mothers, divorcees, and widows.
All members of CFC and the rests of the ministries have gone through the CLP (Christian Life Program, a thirteen week life spirit seminar).

THE HANDMAIDS OF THE LORD

We are members of the CFC Handmaids of the LORD
And CFC means Couples For CHRIST,
Handmaids of the LORD we are called, "H.O.L.D." for short;
And H.O.L.D. is one of the CFC's ministries.

The strong bonding that the handmaids have
is overwhelming and amazing
The fellowship is freely spirit flow
Glamorous faces and smiles glowing through

The secret of all these amazing ladies
is we have a wonderful Immaculate model
Our Blessed Mother, a virgin, a martyr
who brought to the world, our wonderful LORD

So you can imagine the virtues you can have
Faithfulness, Obedience, Humility, and Holiness
Be Handmaids of the LORD if you will
Let us say, "Let it be done to me according
to your Word."

As I've mentioned in the previous page we are members of the H.O.L.D. (Handmaids of the LORD). I used to be a member and every first part of the year we have this "Evangelization Rally, wherein we have ministry cheers for our goals for that year. I have this cheer for the H.O.L.D. in 2005. The phrase Go for the GOLD" represents 50 States that we would like to evangelize.

HANDMAIDS OF THE LORD . . . CHEERS

The Handmaids of the LORD are here to proclaim
the goals for the ministry and HOLD is the name
The goal for GOLD is at hand to be claimed
The Handmaids will go as far as they can
Hooray! Hooray! Glorify GOD's name!
Hooray! Hooray! Glorify GOD's name!

Today is the day to rally again,
to show our LORD our love for His work;
To focus our minds on our missions and goals.
Go! Handmaids Go! For the Gold!
Hooray! Hooray! Glorify GOD's name!
Hooray! Hooray! Glorify GOD's name!

First part of the year is CLP on the line
Chicago's target is from five to nine.
suburbs' is the same, both HOLDs will be fine
Here comes '05 new members will sign.
Hooray! Hooray! Glorify GOD's name!
Hooray! Hooray! Glorify GOD's name!

O LORD our GOD, our Everything
Bless the CFC and the ministries under
We lift up our missions and goals in Your Hand,
empower us please with Your love and warmth
Hooray! Hooray! Glorify GOD's name!
Hooray! Hooray! Glorify GOD's name!

Kathy is one of the clients at the Nursing Home where I used to work. She is so sweet and huggable young lady and smiles all the time. She is legally blind.

KATHY AND SIFTY

There is a young lady with a friend name "Sifty,"
Katherine is her name, likes to say, "Soissidy."
They understand each other with their own language
Love connects them, that's true friendship.

Sifty is Kathy's baby in her mind she is pretty,
If you ask her, she'll tell you that Sifty is blue,
yellow and a beauty;
Kathy sees things and speaks from her heart,
Cares for everyone and especially for Sifty,
So get to know my friend Kathy, one cuddly lady
I honor this woman though she's legally blind,
Her out look in life is positive and bright.

*One of my nieces celebrated her eighteenth birthday
on June 26, the year 2005. She is the second daughter
of Lourna and Robert B. Jimenez. Robert is my third brother.
The celebrant's name is Miss Joyce Elizabeth M. Jimenez*

MY NIECE, A DEBUTANTE

Time has now come to witness one of the
important days of your life,
Your eighteenth birthday, yes you're
a debutante.
It seemed just yesterday, when I saw you
crawling, learning few words, progressed
to climbing, then, walking independently.
You were then a cute little girl,
and now, a very beautiful maiden.
I admire you for your strong character and
strong determination
You are so witty and smart
You are thoughtful in a special way
And you have a way of showing your
compassion.
I witness your great enthusiasm, in studying
and pursuing a higher level of career.
I love you my dear niece and I am proud of you.

THE EIGHTEENTH

A birthday gift that I can give, a poem about life,
a precious gift, and this is dedicated for all
young ladies, who are celebrating their blooming
age, their "eighteenth".
Today is an important day for you,
the start of your blossom youth
Today is a day to remember
and someday you'll have something to ponder.
Life is too short, let's not make it shorter
live your life to the fullest
and do the best thing you can
Just always remember that, there is Somebody
Who will guide you every step of the way,
And it's our LORD JESUS that holds your hands,
And provides you your special angel;
So enjoy your life, be strong in your faith
Always ask GOD's grace in every move you make
May GOD bless you and be with you always.

I wrote this in 2001 when Chikoy was 8 years old. He really was a very assertive little boy and was a very good dancer. He could choreograph other kids too if there was a dance presentation. He even danced in front of the clients in the Nursing Home. He is 18 years old now and still smart, sweet, and a thoughtful young man . . .

CHIKOY

He is eight, he is cute, he is a boy
He has three first names but goes for Chikoy
Francis, John, Angelo his baptismal name,
Yes, that's my nephew and our last name
is the same.

He came to visit the United States
Where me, his aunt stays; he easily
picked up things including the language
He is smart, intelligent, witty little kid.

He is artistic, creative in his own ways
He does write me a letter with crafty inserts
He is good in creating origami stuff
He is something else, I tell you that's
my nephew.

He is so thoughtful and caring
a big heart he has with his tiny being
He likes to hug and kiss every step of the way,
He is always saying, "I love you," "I miss you"
without delay.

He dances good, he has a nice voice
His songs are music and not noise
He has a sense of humor and can make faces,
He can make people laugh of all ages.

He likes to read books and likes to solve mazes
Puzzles, trivia questions he likes to answer,
He is very polite, diplomatic, surprising for his age,
I am glad to have him for short moments.

Chikoy, we will miss you, nanay, your mom
and your dad
Thank you for making your ninang Beth and me
happy and glad
Come back next time and we'll have more fun
Take care my nephew and study well, remember
we love you and will miss you as well.

*(In our dialect (Tagalog) nanay means mother and
ninang means godmother).*

CHINI

I wrote this in 2002. She's 15 years old now, still smart, but prettier and wittier. She receives a lot of medals of honor and recognition. Because of the numbers of medals she has, I teased her to lend them to me since I live in a windy city Chicago, it'll help me stay in one place, if I put all the medals on my neck and I could anchor my feet to the ground and I won't be blown away by the wind . . . She's funny too, telling me that she is already tired of going up the stage to claim her medals.

I have a niece named Esther Charisse
She'll be seven years old this year, a day
after Christmas;
She is pretty, witty and smart,
We call her "Chini" for short
She is sensitive, sweet and inquisitive
Questions she asked, you better be careful
in your response
She reasons logically at her age, it's unusual
Everybody loves my niece and what proud
parents she has
Even though we are apart, seldom seen in flesh
our hearts are connected and spiritually we
are bonded
I can see her growing-up through our conversation
over the phone, it is a spiritual connection.
Chini is my inspiration, like the rests of my
nieces and nephews,
I love them all dearly, from my heart everyone
is a favorite,

I thank the LORD, for all these gifts, the gift of
family, gift of nephews and nieces.
Chini, a prayerful kid and very thankful too,
for the gifts she has received.
Chini, you are an intelligent girl
You are polite, thoughtful and caring little person
I pray that you'll be the same when you reach
the age eighteen
I know my dear you'll be a beautiful maiden.
Again, thank You LORD, for all the children
in this world.

I have written this poem for someone I care about so much. Prayers and big listening ears are my only ways of showing my love for my cherished blood-related person. I would like to remain these moments of pains between her and me, and between her and our Almighty. As this poem is about to be in the book, she is well now and totally healed from the past.

WHAT MUST I DO?

What must I do, now that you left me?
You left me with the aching heart
With the pain that doesn't stop
With the memories that always linger
With the sleepless nights and
overflowing tears.
I am struggling to cope with these
moments of fears,
Fear of the unknown and
Fear of no one to love me again
And fear of doing things against my will.
The only consolation I have at the
moment is, the "love "of the people
around me, especially my parents.
The love that is unconditional and pure
The love that I learn from the One
Whom I was created
Yes, the Image I have now is the
GOD's Image;
Hence I know now, what I must do;
That is to offer everything including my
pains and sorrow to our LORD JESUS
Whom I must trust, my now and tomorrow;
My LORD and my GOD, in You I trust
my life.

TO MY SISTER LINDA

We never get the chance to be closer
We seldom have a confrontation
We only communicate long distance
But now we were given the chance
to bond even for a short time
Both of us wished to bond since childhood
And now, both of us were called to serve
our LORD and that's better.
Lately, while I was recalling your prayers
and praying over me, I can't help but cry.
You are indeed a great sister and a friend
I witnessed how you care for your family
And I honor you for that.
The spiritual tenacity you received from
The Holy Spirit makes you stronger
The fortitude, the obedience, the wisdom and
many more gifts, are your weapons for your
daily endeavors and indeed you are blessed.
Before I go back to the States,
I want you to know, I am very appreciative
of your care and love and I thank you
for being there all the time
I love you sis and keep it up, (the being you)
My loving sister, my best friend.

The names mentioned here are my nephews, nieces and grandchildren. They are our family treasures . . .

OUR FAMILY TREASURES

What a joy and delight having Christian (CJ) in our lives
A little boy less than two years old, our first grandchild
He is so sweet knows a lot of wits
He seldom talks, but very active and expressive

Rona Liza, my maiden niece, a beautiful lady
My buddy, my assistant, my security
She takes care of me, when we're out on spree
She is a full grown woman now, very pretty.

Ralph, another nephew of mine is a grown-up too
Very conscious of himself, very neat and handsome
He always asks if I need help for some errands
He is now on job hunting, pretty soon, he'll land one.

Jan Carlo, the only son of my sister
Witty, independent and very resourceful
Good-looking guy with good personality and likes
to explore the world of computer, let him be.

Joyce Elizabeth, a teenager, a young lady
Walks like a model and likes to be one
She is assertive, open-minded and frank,
Mind you she'll be a compassionate and a very
good nurse.

Paul Christian, the only son of my brother
Very handsome, tall and still a teenager
Likes to play basketball, athletic young boy
He'll be in college two years from now.

Chikoy, the only child of another brother of mine
He stays with me in the States for a short time
He is always one of the tops in Academic class
Talented, creative kid, and I'm proud of him.

Chini, another top kid in school, my youngest niece
Very studious, responsible kid, surprising for her age
She is inquisitive, wants answers for all her queries?
A young kid like her will have a bright future.

Jeje, the oldest among my nephews and nieces
The father of Christian Jay and Elaiza Jelyn,
A loving, thoughtful and responsible husband
He is the very first nephew and first grandchild

Elaiza, the sister of CJ and both my grandchildren
They are the kids of Jeje and Evelyn
A chubby seven months old baby with a sweet smile
Yes, she is so far the 2nd youngest member of the family.

This stanza is a late entry, for I didn't want to miss
To mention another great grandkid;
His name is Jacob Kristoffer, who just celebrated
His first year birthday this June 1st,
The son of Rona and Toffer Sagun and
So far the youngest in the entire clan.

These are my favorites in the family
I am proud of them and I'll tell you truly
I don't have kids, I never had a chance
They are my gifts from GOD, Our Family Treasures.

The late entry was written (May 24,2011), for the new members of the family, (Toffer Sagun and Jacob Kristoffer.

THE SHARED MOMENTS

I flew thousands of miles to see my loved ones
to spend quality moments with them
to bond with each other, to feel GOD's
Presence in one another.
I am glad and overwhelmed with the
moments shared with my family
I am thankful and grateful for the chance
to hug, to kiss and to embrace them freely.
We are blessed to celebrate the gift of life
the 75th birthday of our loving mother
the 59th wedding anniversary of my parents
the 25th wedding anniversary of
Robert and Lourna
the 9th wedding anniversary of Rey and Arleen
the 54th birthday of Linda
and the celebration of my homecoming
all this we are thankful for
And GOD is so good GOD and awesome.
The moments we shared must never be forgotten
the shared moments must be treasured forever
We thank GOD for everything including the
moments of bonding
Yes I will always ponder the time I spent with
my wonderful family
In my heart I will treasure the love and care
we poured out on each other.
And through GOD's blessings and graces
we attained harmonious relationship
and for that I am ever grateful.
Thank You LORD for uniting us not only in
Spirit but in flesh.
Thank You LORD for being in our midst
Most of all, thank You for the moments
we shared
Yes, the shared moments are the moments
of love and peace.

This is a special request from a person I met in the Craft Show. I just asked her the things she likes to remember about her grandfather, and here it is a short poem for her to honor her grandfather. I wished I have known my grandfather in flesh. I didn't see my grandfather from both sides of the family, but I knew I have two great ones.

A GRANDFATHER

The memories with my grandfather are vivid
The laughter we share and the books he reads
The stories he tells, have moral lessons
I am proud of my grandfather, he is the best.
A grandfather is someone you can trust
Yes, my grandfather is always defending us
And he is just
I love you grandfather from my heart I say
I will treasure the moments we shared together.

Since I have written a poem for a grandfather for someone, I thought of writing poems for grandmother, father, mother, daughter, son, sister and brother.
They will be in the following pages.
This particular poem is based on the story of one of my friends, who was brought up by her grandmother.
For me, I owe my education from my grandmother. She was the one who supported me in my studies. I became a nurse because of her. I love you "lola"

A GRANDMOTHER

A grandmother is someone who cares and shares
A grandmother is someone who listens attentively
A grandmother is someone we can lean on
When things in our lives go wrong
I thank my grandmothers for having our parents
But most of all, I thank GOD for creating
Grandmothers, especially my own grandmothers
Who are always there at all times
I honor you and love you both, my special grandmas.

This was written on June of 2002 a tribute to all fathers (living and deceased.) Happy Father's Day to all, especially our GOD the Father in Heaven.

A FATHER'S VOW

The father is the man in the family
He is known as the "bread winner,"
He makes the family happy
He is a lifetime partner of a mother
A father works hard to make a living
to provide for the family needs
He takes care of their being
like taking care of the sprouting seeds
A father is the strong image being seen
He is the foundation of his children
He looks after the children's protection
He is a family oriented and devoted person.
But a father is sensitive too
And needs the love and care
Children must give their share, by
being respectful and obedient as well
A father's vow is very clear
that is to give his love and care
to be faithful to his wife
as he promised in his life and the vow
to be together "till death do us part."
But the best vow that we should know
is the vow of our Father, the Almighty
The vow of His love and mercy
That is from here to eternity.

*This was written on Father's Day 2010, my utmost
reverence to the BEST and GREATEST FATHER
in the universe, Our Father in Heaven.
ABBA FATHER, PAPA JESUS, THE NAME ABOVE ALL NAMES . . .
Happy Father's Day to You, the Father of all.*

THE FATHER I KNOW

He is there when I needed Him
He is here, there and everywhere
He is available at all times
He is the Father I know.

He cares for my feelings
He touches my heart
He knows all my thoughts
He is the Father I know.

He listens to my sighs
He shows me the way
He guides me in my action
He is the Father I know.

He keeps all the promises
He gives me gifts that last
He lifts my heart with joy
He is the Father I know.

He carries my burden
He forgives my wrong doings
He grants me His love and mercy
He is the Father I know.

The Father I know is the Father you know
What He does for me, He does for you
He is the Father of your fathers
And everyone else, so today let us
Give honor and greet them,
"Happy Father's Day."

FATHER

I know I seldom say, "I love you"
But in my heart I do
A father like you I do honor
For you are my great mentor
When I am in trouble
You always bail me out
You give me encouraging words
Words of wisdom to go on
Without you father, my life is a mess
I thank you for guiding me every
step of the way
And letting me know the right pathway
Father, I'll treasure my moments
with you and I love you forever.

A MOTHER

A mother is someone who cares so much
of her siblings and pour out her love
unconditionally;
A mother is someone you can turn to
when things go wrong
A mother is someone who bears the pain
for the sake of her children
A mother is a friend, a mentor and a confidant
She is indeed, "Jack of all trades," a great
decent vocation
A mother is someone to be honored and be
remembered forever.
But there is a great mother who prays
all the time, intercede for us and with us
She's the sinless ever virgin Mother Mary,
the model of all mothers and motherhood.

*A friend of mine is the chairman of an organization and
she had a fund raising and held in May. In this occasion
(Mother's Day) she presented the mothers to be honored
for their accomplishments in life.
My friend requested me to write something about mothers.
HAPPY MOTHER'S DAY to all Mothers (living and deceased.)*

A MOTHER'S HEART

There's nothing in this world a mother can't do
To show her love for her kids;
There's nothing she won't do to survive
her motherhood;
There's enough love in her heart to offer
a great deal,
So a mother's heart is indeed real.

Did we ever for a moment recall the time
she spent when we were young?
The warm touch, the caring words and
the lullabies she sang?
When we were sick, didn't you know that
her heart bleeds?
So what really is a mother's heart?

Whom do you call when you are in trouble?
When you feel any aches, whose name
comes first?
The first word you learned, what is it?
Yes, "mama" is the word audible in one's ears.
So a mother's heart surely is thrilled.

Many more memories to ponder on
Memories of mothers of our own
So let us be thankful from now on
And thank our LORD GOD for creating
these beautiful and wonderful women,
The mothers with golden crowns.

The Golden Crown is a symbol of our Blessed
Mother Mary, the Ever Virgin, the model
of all mothers.
So let us honor our Blessed Mother this May
A celebration for Mother's Day and her
Crowning Day.
Let us salute all mothers for their enduring
hearts, love and care.
Now, what is a mother's heart again?

A SON

You make us happy, just having you
You color our world and that is true
You bring joy to your sister and brother
You're a model indeed to the youngsters.
You are a very pleasant person
We are indeed proud of you
You give us inspiration, there's such a
Delight in our hearts
Thank you our son for just being you,
A son to be treasured forever.

A DAUGHTER

A lovely girl you turned out to be
A beautiful person that we see
A good pupil who is so studious
That's our daughter, and she is the best
We are proud of you dear daughter
For your performance and behavior
For being a lovable and sweet girl
Yes, our daughter, we love you forever.

MY SISTER, MY FRIEND

I am lucky to have you as my friend
You are indeed a good listener
I thank our parents for having you
You are my best sister and best friend.
When I needed someone to talk to
You are there with open arms
Your warm embrace I surely felt
My sister I love you, most of all as
my best friend.

A BROTHER FOREVER

I can't imagine how grown-up you've been
Sharing the fun together
A brother like you is worth reminiscing
Indeed you are a brother forever.
I missed the time when you pretend
to be a grown-up
Defending me against all odds
I'll treasure every bit of my memories with you
Indeed you are a brother forever
For me you are the best bro and I'll be
loyal forever.

I wrote this when I was in Little Rock, Arkansas in 1974, working as a nurse. I had a dog, (actually still a puppy), and he was my first pet in the United States. And this was my third poem since my high school time. And now I have poems about my other pets. Read them in the following pages.

KISSO

That's my dog, Kisso is his name
With human thoughts, with human feelings
His span of life, nine months this month
It's very short, it breaks my heart.

I didn't know what name to give him
Until he showed his loving behavior
Since it's a boy and loves to kiss
"Kisso" is the name I have given.

One thing I can be proud of, about my dog
Is how he faced the camera and posed
He was playful, funny and tricky
Kisso my dog, I missed him truly.

What is a dog in this world?
Entertainer? A company? A buddy? A playmate?
Or just a common watcher on the porch?
No folks, a dog is a best friend you must know.

Now, it's all over and my Kisso is gone
Nobody is to bark at night
Neither to wake us up at dawn
Poor Kisso, my beloved, thank you for all the fun.

That's my dog, Kisso is his name,
With human thoughts with human feelings
His span of life, nine months this month,
It's very short, it breaks my heart.

*Smarty was the first cat we had here in the U.S.
We got him from the "Adopt-A-Pet" sponsored
by the Anti-Cruelty To Animals. His previous name
was "Seagram" and we changed it to "Smarty."
We got Princess from an old couple. They had about
seven cats. Princess was the most aloof cat we've ever had.
We intended to pick her as a challenge for us to train her
to be friendly. So Princess is the chosen one.*

THE "PURR"-FECT FRIENDS

We have two cute and lovely cats,
Smarty and Princess, but scared of the rats
They are entertaining and playful
Sure they are our purr-fect friends.
Aren't they wonderful?
Smarty thinks he is a dog sometimes
He bites our legs to get attention
He likes to drink milk with daily serving
He is amazing for a feline like him
Princess, is like her name, is a royal feline
Snobbish by nature and picky at times
She hides from our guests, but sneaks to peep
She is an intelligent cat, likes "hide and seek."
Yes, these are our two purr-fect pets,
The purr-fect friends at home
We love them so dearly and cares for them
Smarty and Princess our best companions
Now that they are gone, with their
Fido friend BeeJay,
Their memories are in our hearts forever and
In our hearts they have special place.

As I was driving along Ashland street here in Chicago, I saw a small dog crossing the street. I stopped and I tried to call her (it was a female I found out) and submissively she came to me. I asked around if she was a neighbor dog? No one seemed to know her nor the owner. So, I picked her up and advertised in a local paper of a lost dog. I even distributed my business cards around the area, before I left the place. After two weeks no one called, so we adopted her and gave her a name of Beejay. We had her for at least nine years and we had fun, love and full of unforgettable memories with her.

BEEJAY

Beejay is a peekapoo breed
With beige and white mixed
She likes to talk and has good
eye contact
She dances well with rhythmic steps . . .

Beejay is a good watcher
And she is also a good passenger
She stays in the car and behaves well
She loves joy riding we can tell.

Beejay has a special place in our hearts
We love her dearly and cares for her a lot;
She is gone now and the rests of the gang,
Smarty, Princess and Beejay, you'll
be treasured forever.

THE CROCODILE

Rough skin you have, fascinating creature
You have bulging eyes, I hate to say
But you have an ugly feature
Your eyelids are big, your jaws are long
Your mouth when it's widely open
Is like an entrance of a cave
You swim at sea, crawl on land
What else do you have?
Your tail swing like a baseball bat
You always win in a reptile combat
Your teeth are huge and sharp
You easily can swallow your catch and
have a big burp.
I'm trying to think of something positive
about you,
Ironic it is, but poachers like to kill you
So they can sell and make money out of you
Now I know what to think and say
That you're also GOD's creation, so here
you can stay,
You are useful and valuable, not yet in extinction
Unlike the elephants and some animals, on their
way to oblivion
Kids like to watch you even though you're scary
They study you and learn about you, plenty
I guessed crocodiles are unique, though their harmful.
But I know that everything that GOD created was
beautiful.

*Way back in 1993, I used to collect elephant memorabilia (stuff, figurines, pins, jewelries, even articles and picture clippings, cups/mugs, or anything about elephants.) Recently,
I have submitted a manuscript entitled, "Have Phun With Elefants". It's about elephant jokes, with riddles and knock-knock games. Actually, this was supposed to be my first book. The situation didn't allow me to have it published that early.*

EXTINCTION

We, the elephant herds are pleading
for our lives here in the jungle
It's not a threat, it's not a warning
It's a request, our only angle.

Our lives are in danger constantly,
Watching our back for the unknown entity
The invaders are now in our property
"Poachers", they are called,
the guilty party.

We are begging in behalf of the residents
of the jungle all over,
To respect our rights here on earth
We were created same as you, with
purpose in this world
So do something dear readers to
stop the extinction of our herds.

The poem itself is the story of PERRY

PERRY

We have a dog named Perry, we got him
in the mid nineties, he was six months old,
when we got him, saw him walking on our
lawn covered with snow.
A week after someone was at our door
looking for a puppy, black in color.
Description was right with black spot on
his tongue, that's Perry alright.
Later, we found out he was for sale
They're looking for a buyer
So we did offer to buy him
But we got him free, because the owner
sensed we're fond of him.
His original name was Kenwood
a mature name for a puppy
So we changed it to Perry,
A classy name for a Shih-Tzu puppy.
When we moved to the suburbs
we found out from his vet
that our Perry has Addison's Disease,
a disorder of adrenal glands
and needs a lifetime med
Perry is so sweet, cuddly and affectionate
He knows when we're sad and if we're glad
He sympathized with us in our low moments
and rejoices with our excitement.
He is a very good watcher, friendly
He likes children, he thinks they are related
Tricks are for the dogs, wits are for this dog.
Bless all the pets, dogs and cats
Bless all GOD's creatures.

Another pet goes to heaven. Yes, Perry left us with broken hearts again. Even though Perry had this Addison's Disease, he didn't suffer at his death bed. He had a very playful, fun, and enjoyable life. Thank you LORD for all the animals and pets and for all animal lovers.

MEMORIES TO PONDER

(In memory of Perry)

Nine years, the length of time you spent with us
A candle was added on your cake yearly, t'was a blast
You acted, you behaved like the way we did
You were sweet, loyal, and happy pet.
Your name was Kenwood when we got you
We changed it to Perry, it favored your cute face
"Little Shih-Tzu."
Your doctors liked you and so with your groomer.
There was a report card saying "You're a Talker"
And every time you came from your grooming
You always knew there was a toy for you, waiting.
Your toy was a reward and you knew if it was
a new toy or not.
You loved to play with those squeaky toys
You ran, you charged like in a football player
The squeaky sound was not a noise
because you knew how to create rhythmic notes
There was a spot in our garage that you used when
we walked you out (without a leash) on the lined-up
newspapers and you knew where they're at.
Every time we let you out you knew we would wash
your face, your feet with damp wash cloth afterwards
and you helped us by raising up your legs.

When we put your leash, you knew what door to use
you always went at the front door, not in the garage
You were that intelligent, smart witty Fido
You had few favorite spots inside the house
You often stayed by the porch to watch the neighbor's cat
You liked to view the man-made pond near-by
You chased through your mind the birds, the
rabbits, the mallards around;
You had many more tricks, moves, sounds
for us to ponder on our moments of sadness
We thank GOD for giving you in our lives
We treasure every moment you spent with us
We are grateful too, for you didn't suffer that much
And you were still alert and active at your
last moments
Perry, we would like you to know that we love
you so dearly
And we will miss the fun, the joy and especially
you, truly.
We can only ponder the memories with you,
our huggable Shih-Tzu, Perry.

This poem/letter was placed inside Perry's small casket (made of fiberglass). We had a proper burial for all our pets. We bought lands from the pet lawn and part of the deal is to have a proper burial for the pets. Beejay and Smarty were in one space, Princess and Perry in another space. That's how we loved our pets. We respect them, up to their last moments.

GOOD-BYE OUR PERRY

We thank our LORD for giving, you, Perry
in our lives
And for bringing us into your life
Thank you Perry for the fun memories
Thank you for behaving like a human being
Thank you for consoling us when you see
us crying
Thank you for the nine years of bonding
We are grateful, too, for GOD is with you
till the end
He didn't let you suffer, in spite of your illness
So our beloved Perry, good-bye for now
See you in heaven someday
And extend our love to Cleo, Krypto, Barney,
Princess, Bester, Katrina, Smarty, Snowy and
all the white cats we had and of course Kisso,
Eddie and Beejay
Remember you'll always be in our hearts
We love you truly and you'll be missed a lot.

As it says below, I got him from the suburb Lombard and got his name from that place. My first time to have a pet fish. I've learned that beta-fish span of life is really short. It has been proven true about this information. We had at least four beta-fishes for the two past years and they didn't last long. We'll be missing you Zaber, Cris, Tisoy, and Mindy. You were all adorable, beautiful and of course very colorful fishes.

LOMBARDO, MY BETAFISH

I never knew that a fish like you wanted a solo life
They say you don't get along with other fish, even your own kind
You're so pretty with bluish-purple caudal fin
You swim beautifully, and nibbles neatly
I'm fond of you my dear Lombardo,
And I do always like to talk to you
I got you from the garage sale at Lombard
And that's where I got your name
I just added "O" from that suburb Lombard . . . o!
But the sad thing my dear fish is, you're gone now and forever
I'll treasure every bit of your memory in my heart, my dear fish friend
Lombardo, my beta fish, I'll miss you truly
Thank you for the time you were with me
May GOD Bless all the pets, including you
Lombardo, my beta fish.
I love you little fellow.

Jun and Jean are my brother and sister respectively in CHRIST. They requested me to write something about Cookie, their lovely dog. I gathered the information about him and there it was, Cookie. I wrote this in October of 2002. I met Cookie personally and he likes me. He is a people dog. I haven't seen them for quite a while.

COOKIE

We have a dog named, "Cookie",
We had her since the year ninety three
She is cute breed dog and so lovely
We are happy to have her as a family
Now that our own kids are grown-ups
And have place of their own
We have Cookie left with us to share
The love at home.
Cookie is not an ordinary pet
She is a dog that can pray and praise
Making sounds while people are praying
Howling in a subtle way, while others
are singing.
When there is a Christian Life Program
She is also wearing a name tag that it says,
"Dog For CHRIST"
We are indeed proud of this angel pet
And we treat her as one of our kids
So Cookie this is for you, from your
Mommy, Daddy, Christine and Tony.
Thank you for you're not only our best
Friend, but being part of the family.

As it says below, my brother Robert scooped him from the small nearby lake, and I knew he was meant to be my new reptile pet. On the next page is a poem about Pong, but he is the one reciting the poem. By the way, "Pagong" is the translation of turtle in our country, Philippines.

MY PET "PONG"

Summer of 2004, I was with my brother
at the small lake nearby;
We were fishing and the waves frequently
moving towards where we're at,
prompted by the breezy wind.
Not much of a fishing that time
But there was a tiny creature
swimming towards us.
Robert, with his big hand scooped
this little thing, a tiny turtle sized of a teaspoon;
I named him "Pong", like a turtle cartoon
in our country, (Philippines.) (Pong-Pagong)
Now, Pong is about the size of a tablespoon
and still growing slowly.
I didn't know that a turtle like Pong, responds
to human care, maybe its rare.
I guess if you treat any creature with warmth
and love, in return will show some affection.
Pong can distinguish the food he prefers;
If I show the green cap cover, he would just
swim away and around
But if it's a yellow cap cover, he would poke
the glass and would widely open his mouth.
Sometimes he is like a bird with very small
beak, snapping the food from my fingers.
I enjoy his company by talking to him,
cleaning his dwelling place, feeding him and
letting him walk once a day around a certain
part of the house, which I could feel he enjoys.
Yes, that's my dearly new pet, Pong, a tiny turtle.

*This poem was written two years after we found Pong.
I didn't realize that a turtle can do some tricks too.
As the years go by, Pong learned to follow me while
I walked around the house. One day, I discovered that
he can dance, lifting his body up like tip-toeing and
he does this while I hum. We even video taped him.
He thinks he is a person. We are really fond of him,
to the extent of me, writing a book about him, entitled,
"202 Turtle Haiku". I just submitted the manuscript
few weeks ago. So wait for the coming of Pong's book.*

THAT'S ME PONG

Walk, walk, walk, that's me Pong
exploring the world
Don't you know, I carry a heavy load?
I can look at you face to face and
My better viewing is side to side
Though I'm the slowest creature on earth
I am persistent, witty and patient.
And I am a climber, a dancer, a thinker,
and an achiever.
Splash, splash, splash, that's me
taking a bath and at the same time
having my snack
I can only have my meals in the water.
Ooops! I have a name, my rescuer
calls me "Pong:" She saved me from
the claws of the vulture.
Now, I've grown into the size of a
cell phone, that's me "Pong."

The poem itself is the whole story of our Benjie,
our dog celebrity. We have Benjie for four years now.

"BENJIE"

Four years after Perry passed away
we thought of having a dog again.
He is not from the pound
Mind you, he is not a stray.

We didn't intend to have a pet again
but I have set a standard to follow
that if I can see a five color Shih-Tzu
There goes my vote, to the right fellow.

Through the internet search, there was a match
A five color Shih-Tzu came out;
A family from Iowa is breeding this kind
We didn't waste time, we ordered one.

From the airport cargo, we picked him up
It says, "Abner" his name in the tag
He was glad, seeing his tail wagged
We are glad too, we welcome him with warmth.

We decided to name him "Benjie",
From the famous dog celebrity
He is so cute, sweet and friendly, but
There is a distinctive feature he has,
His tongue is longer than the norm
Long or not, we love him so much.

One thing amazing is, Benjie doesn't like treats
So we aren't worried, he doesn't need to diet.
He is within the normal weight
He takes care of his own health

He jumps so high like the one in the Animal Planet
He reaches the door knob and higher than that
He loves to eat at the same time we do
He is a self-teaching/learning trick dog too.

He knows how to ask for his food, but never
begs when we are eating, that he understood.
He barks if he wants to drink water
And he is good in watching our turtles.

He knows there are other pets in the house
He makes sure it is not a mouse
He doesn't like the sound of the scratches
And he barks thinking he is protecting
the turtles.

Benjie is a cuddly, friendly and sweet doggie
He likes to pull out our hair rhythmically
He thinks it's a massage of the scalp and he likes
To be massaged too and fall asleep afterwards.

Our Benjie thinks he is the favorite
It is true, he is one of the favorite pets (except)
for Pong (the turtle), a favorite too,
We love him dearly and he is cutie
For us he is therapy.

Benjie loves to play with children
And he has two smart best friends
Andi and MJ are their names, they like to pat
him and do a "trick or treat" on Halloween.

So my dear readers, if you have a pet and
want to treat him extra nice, write a short story
about him or say something good and deserving.
Benjie, thank you our faithful friend Shih-Tzu
a real being.

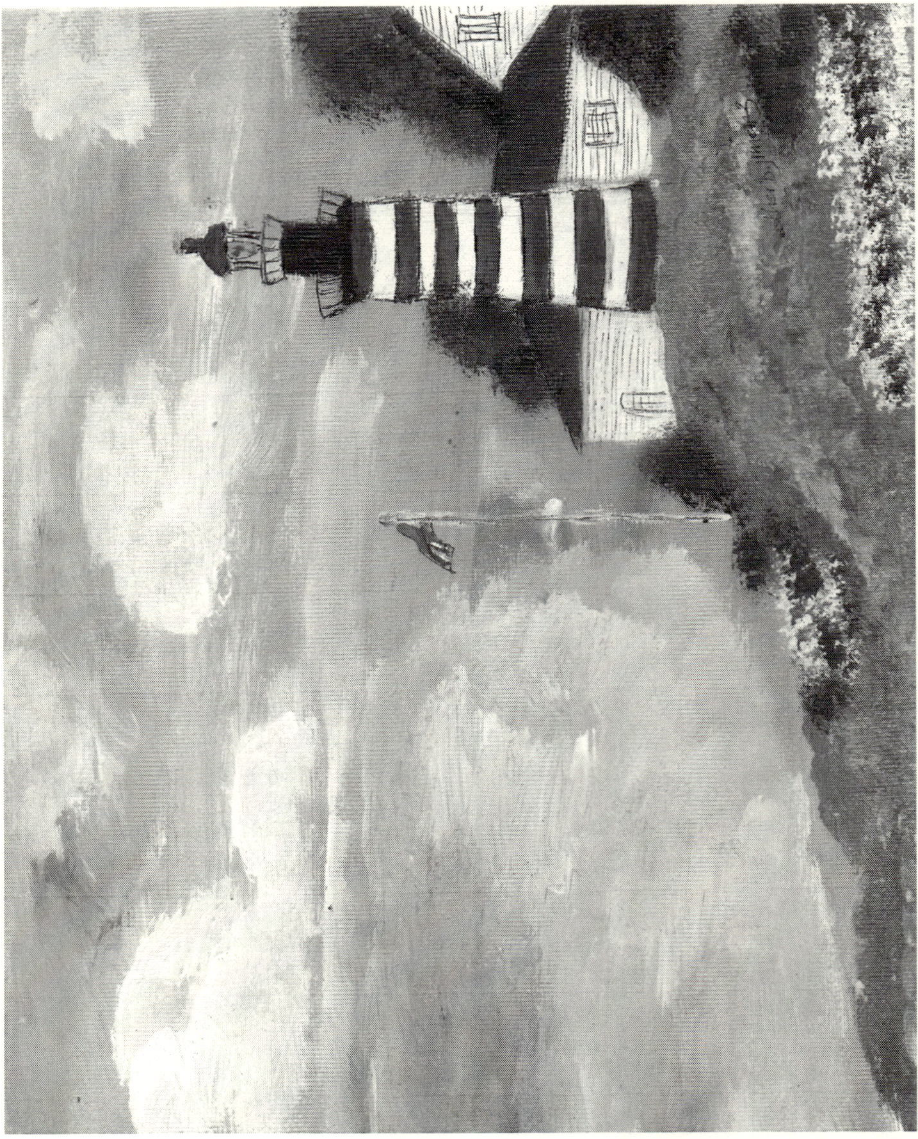

CHAPTER III
POEMS FOR THE SEASON

Some States have four seasons, some don't have. It's so happened that I am in the States with four seasons. I get the chance to witness the beauty of changing climates, clothes attire, the variety of activities (outdoor and indoor,) and many more. Just imagine going with the flow of four seasons, the tulips in Springtime, the Summer extravaganzas, the raking of golden, yellow, brown leaves in Autumn, and the soft, delicate looking snows in Winter.

Poems for the season are not only the physical aspect of it. You will be informed of the essence of holiday seasons, the celebrations of the important events and many more happenings. Life is too short and let's make the most of it. Feel the changes around you and you will see the changing you. Be ready to tune in yourself with the seasons in life and enjoy the seasons of your heart.

CHRISTMAS IS NOT X-MAS

I know you're rushing, I know you're busy
I know it's easier to write X-mas in
your greetings
But let's see who is missing?
CHRIST it is, not seen, because you
only wrote X, before the "mas" thing.
X is unknown, X is elimination
But we know who CHRIST JESUS is
and we don't want to eliminate Him, do we?
So the right thing to do next time you hold
your pen is, to write the complete word,
CHRISTMAS, and this is the simplest
and most valuable gifts we can give our
Creator, because JESUS CHRIST is the
Reason for this season!

CHRISTMAS IS . . . LOVE

Once there was a secret love
A love that comes in season
A love that gives chill to all
A love that is all over the world
Yes, that is Christmas love, a love
That is for everyone.

Christmas love is contagious
Christmas love is extravagant
Christmas seems short
And Christmas love is the love
That brings peace and joy.

Christmas love shouldn't be a secret
Christmas love must not be seasonal
Christmas love brings not only chills
But warmth
Christmas love must be in our hearts
Yes, Christmas love is JESUS in every
Essence of Word and Being
And he is the very reason for this season.

BEYOND CHRISTMAS

Is Christmas over, may I ask?
The afterglow of Christmas
is beyond that
It is only the beginning of
knowing our LORD
The sole owner of our souls and
this world.

Our LORD Almighty didn't
stop His works
He is always there to show His
mercy and love
He guides everyone every step
of the way
He gives us our Advocate as
our companion everyday.

If we can only focus our mind
beyond Christmas
We will discover the virtues at hand
for CHRIST JESUS will be
forever in our hearts
And the Christmas will be celebrated
all through out.

"Yes my beloved children," as our
LORD will say,
"Feel me now and in your heart, I'll stay
And my Son JESUS, I'll give to all, today
This is my beyond Christmas gift
A gift to be treasured forever."

IT'S CHRISTMAS ONCE AGAIN

The chilly Winter welcomes the holidays
The snow can't wait to show off again
The stores around are loaded with displays
The kids check Santa's lists of names
It's Christmas once again.

The Christmas trees enjoy their lights
and ornaments
The Christmas cards are delivered
and received
The traditions observed here and there
Ho! Ho! Ho! Santa's voice is heard
It's Christmas once again.

Exchange gifts among families and friends
Christmas songs heard and sang
Going to church hearing the mass
Reverence for the Greatest Celebrant
It's Christmas once again.

Yes, celebration of Christmas season is
overwhelming
And sometimes we forget the other beings
The ones in the battle (the brave soldiers in uniform)
The ones who are poor and who indeed
Have nothing.

Once again let's not focus too much
on ourselves
Let us ponder on the future works of JESUS
Let us bring homage and glad tidings
to the poor
And let us keep our war heroes in our prayers
It's Christmas once again.

Once again let's live a simple life with our
faith and love
A life full of prayers and hope
A life that knows forgiveness
And a life that is CHRIST-centered
It's Christmas once again.

THE BALLAD OF THE SHEPHERDS

Walking on the open fields
Tending the flocks of sheep
Wearing dirty torn clothes
Guiding the sheep on the road
These were the shepherds
The lowly of all as we're told.
The recipients of the most
Important message in the world
The angel's voice, loud and clear
We've heard, shout for joy for
CHRIST JESUS is here on the
stable where he lays with other
beautiful creatures watching.
"Glory to GOD, Good Tidings and
Peace on Earth"
These were the Good News heard by
the humble shepherds
Blessed are the shepherds, who first
witnessed the Holy Family
the first to honor and worship
the family reverently
the first mankind to pay homage
to the New Born King in swaddling
clothes, to the Greatest Man, to the
One who will save us all
Let us rejoice and glorify our
Sovereign King
This is the Ballad of the Shepherds
From their hearts they humbly sing.

THE CHRISTMAS CARDS

Beautiful cards receive from the mails
Pictures of nativity are top on the list
Amazing artists with gifted hands
Share their talents all over the world
All these you can see in the Christmas cards.
Winter scenes, snows on the roof
Snows on the branches of trees
Ice skating, sleigh riding, ice skiing
with heavy coats, warm boots
knitted scarves and bonnets
All these you can see in the Christmas cards.
Three kings on the camels, guided by the star
with three wonderful gifts on their hands
these are all for the newborn babe
A beautiful baby boy in the stable
and humble shepherds profoundly
paying homage
All these you can see in the Christmas cards.
From now on pay attention to the Christmas
cards you received
Ponder on each character scene.
Pretend you're in the picture visiting
our Creator
The one who saves us, the Divine Savior
Christmas or not, please save those cards
for you to ponder once in a while
And the Spirit of Christmas will be
forever in your hearts.

THE SPIRIT OF CHRISTMAS

The magic of Christmas is the feeling of
joy and delight
The season seems to last for more months
The children expect gifts from Santa Claus
The shoppers are busy roaming around
The eggnogs, the hot coco, the chestnuts
and the marshmallows are served
the champagne toast, the cheers for
the New Year
The traditions practice by different cultures
These are the effects of Christmas spirit
The Spirit of Christmas is within us
Because it's the birthday of CHRIST JESUS
And we should always remember
to put in our hearts and thoughts
that JESUS is the reason for this season
And He is the genuine Spirit of Christmas.

EXCHANGE OF GIFTS

One of the traditions at Christmas time is
Exchange of gifts
We do this among families-relatives
and friends
The giving and receiving is a wonderful
feeling
But let's go deeper to the exchange
gifts meaning.

When JESUS was born in Bethlehem
The shepherds paid homage to the King
The Good News was given for all mankind
Awareness of salvation has begun.

Our LORD JESUS CHRIST gives us the
Greatest gift
That is to save us for our sins
In return we must give Him a simple gift
To know Him more and imitate His deeds
And that is the greatest exchange of gifts.

GOOD, BETTER, BEST

Santa Claus myth, must be respected
Santa is popular all over the world
Children of younger ages expect more gifts
But you better be good or else
It's nice to be good and be good all the time
But it is better to extend another mile
If you do these in the length of time
The best of you is the image you've grown
Good, better, best, three virtuous qualities
These are the things we need on earth
And just ponder on these three things
And use these as guides for your resolutions
One thing we should remember is, who
Real Santa is?
He is none other than the Newborn King
The Best and Greatest Giver of all
So, be good, be better until you become the best.
The best not of all but the best of yourself.

ADVENT

'Tis the time of the year to smile
A smile that lasts a little longer
For a new born babe is here again
The baby that will save us forever.
In the midst of our busy hour
Let's not forget the essence of advent
Its true meaning and what its message
And let's welcome in our hearts our
LORD JESUS.
'Tis the time to forgive and be forgiven
A sweet reconciliation, a happy reunion
This is the start and let's prepare for the
New beginning
Why don't we do this through out the
Year, better off forever.

PREPARE THE WAY, WE MUST

Prepare the way, we must
To welcome our LORD JESUS
Prepare the way, we must
To show our love and trust
Prepare the way, we must . . . forgive
And ask for forgiveness
We must prepare the way for our GOD
By straightening our life
Through our repentance
And doing GOD's will
Through His grace and through our endurance
We will have the best preparation
For this season of invitation
That's the essence of Advent
So let us prepare the way
For JESUS is the reason for the season.

SEASONS IN MY HEART

Clouds at night so clear
Seemed engulfing a certain
portion of the land
Cold, chilly flowing
melt as it reaches the ground
Mallards are dancing
With the tune of silent snow
No doubts it's still Winter
Few yellows, reds and golden ones
Slowly touching the green grass
Brown and orange follows
Faded leaves falling
Raking time is here again
Burning bush, fiery
Wild flowers, tulips
Bees, busy buzzing, flirting
with the sweet bloomers.
Fresh rain wants to play
Flowers witness the rivalry
of the sprouting buds
Drought, humid, thirsty
Basking turtles, fishing time
Sunrise, sunset, hot
Reflection of water
Glaring, daring, face to face
The mirror of itself . . .
Seasons in my heart.

THE CHRISTMAS WITHIN US

What is the essence of the season?
Of the season to celebrate
To celebrate the most important event
The event to be remembered
Is that the Christmas within us?

The spirit of Christmas is contagious
Contagious as to the feelings of joy
and delight
Delight to feel the coming of the
Triumphant JESUS
JESUS, the Savior of mankind
Is that the Christmas within us?

The warm and the cold, the breeze
And the wind
The mixed temp of the city scene
The scene of the busy mall, full of lights
Full of lights, full of love in the
Shopper's hearts
Is that the Christmas within us?

The symbols of Christmas is outpouring
Outpouring with heartfelt yearning
Yearning for the baby in a manger
In a manger where the Baby JESUS lay
Is that the Christmas within us?

The caroling, the sound of the bells
the singing of the Christmas songs
The Christmas songs felt in the heart
in the heart of all, the rhythm of joy
The joy and the scent of Christmas in the air
Is that the Christmas within us?

The Christmas tradition is practiced
Practiced mostly all over
The exchange of gifts is one of them
One of them is a many
A many, a few, a less or more
Christmas is enough to celebrate by all
And Christmas should always be within us.

The most essential thing in life is not
Seasonal but spiritual
The coming of JESUS is not a symbol
But lasting love offered to us all
"So my dearest mankind," says the LORD
"Have A Blessed Christmas!"
"Here is my Gift, my Beloved Son,
Your LORD CHRIST JESUS."
Thank You my LORD for the Christmas
within us.

FOUR SEASONS

First part of the year is half-winter
Half-spring . . . January still cold,
Still snowing . . . April, the fourth month
flowers start blooming, but surprisingly
We can't tell where the weather is going.

Second quarter is between chilly
and warm, and the visiting rain,
floods in some places, and with a
tornado warning and a real twister.
But June is the month to do most of
the outing.

Third quarter we should never miss
This is the start of the changing colors
of the leaves from great trees
And on the ground they fall
Fall season is what it is called
And sometimes it's called Autumn.

Are we going back then, for a winter
turn, to witness a snow storm?
And the shoveling team?
It's the last month of the year
the completion of the fourth quarter
And December comes, few months
before Spring again.

The nice thing to live in a place with
Four seasons is, you can look forward
For the weather changes, you get to
wear seasonal clothes, that will suit
the weather and be comfortable.

Four seasons affect the people's ways
of living
Goals are varied, to fit the weather
Enjoy whatever season comes your way
Because Spring, Summer, Fall and
Winter are also GOD's wonderful creations.

BEGIN THE NEW YEAR

Let Us . . .
Begin the New Year with an attitude of gratitude
Begin the New Year by going extra mile with a smile
Begin the New Year with self-discipline to focus
on goals to attain
Begin the New Year with perseverance and patience
with the families and friends
Begin the New Year with truth and honesty to be free
of guilt and stress free
Begin the New Year with the Christian ways to
attain more virtues and graces.
And begin the New Year with everything at your best
Remember you can only do these beginnings
with GOD's grace
So begin the New Year by acknowledging in your
life, GOD's Presence.

THE NEWNESS IN US

Another year to face
Another year to praise
Another year to huddle
Another year to ponder
Another year of challenge
Another year of essence
Another year for goals
Another year to ball
Another year of the newness in us.

Every year is a new start
Every year is a change of heart
Every year is a new beginning
Every year is a change of being
Every year are more changes
So another year of the newness in us.

The newness in us is a way to peace
The newness in us is a blessing from GOD
The newness in us is the key to success
The newness in us is a self-awareness
Yes, the newness in us is another year
to treasure
A year to be aware of the Presence
of our Almighty GOD in our lives
and to remain in our hearts forever!

NEW BEGINNING

The time is here again to welcome another year
To start a new life, new beginning
Many resolutions in our minds to put into actions
It is only through oneself, where the resolutions happen.

We can be better if we try our best
And we can settle with what we have
Let's be content of who we are
Remember, we are created in GOD's Image.

One of the things you can do this year
is to have a helping hand and to extend few miles
You won't sweat doing this, but you will gain
a few points
Points you can save for a better future.

Be kind, have compassion and speak gently
You will live your life pleasant and fully
Your list of resolutions, just put them in your heart
Just start the year with the good new beginning.

THE PARISH MISSION NIGHTS

Three consecutive nights, the parish mission has, to gather
the parishioners, guests and everyone, to listen, to watch
and to participate in the mission plan.
Yes, this was used to be our parish church, St. Peter, the
Apostle in Itasca.
St. Peter church is proud and honored to have Fr. Michael
Sparough, to conduct, to teach and to instill in our hearts,
the power of parables as played through.
Yes, the three nights are not just ordinary nights,
But three nights, the unforgettable moments in our lives.
We learned the essence of signing our faith,
"In the name of the Father, and the of the Son and the
Holy Spirit."
And from our hearts, we fervently say the "Our Father,"
the meaning, not only to utter but with the Holy gesture.
We are blessed through the ritual blessings
and we feel the power of the Holy Spirit within
What a wonderful way to spend our lent days
to prepare ourselves, before the Holy Easter
to ponder in our hearts the value of discipleship,
and the gift of reconciliation that we must receive.
And not to forget the true mission that we must fulfill,
to spread the Good News, the Word of GOD,
the true meaning of redemptive suffering and ransoming
of our sins, the chance to be co-evangelist with the
Apostles that He had anointed
All this we are thankful and grateful, and I pray in
Jesus name, Amen!

SOUP AND SALAD

At the entrance of the church posted
for sign ups, for the soup and salad
every Friday night
Some signed up for specific pot-luck
Some monetary, and they are all
contributions from the heart
Many parishioners signed-up, individual
or group
This is done every year, during
Lent season
Great idea to have this fellowship
and light meal shared
Another idea to volunteer the service
Nice to see familiar faces
Some names known, some not
Each one has a name tag attached
to be acquainted more
The dining hall is properly arranged,
each table has small triple crosses and with
tea lights lit, giving the feeling of solemnity.
We have our two parishioner priests with us
We are really blessed with this special gift
GOD Bless our priests and the parishioners
of St. Peter, the Apostle.

FORTY DAYS OF LENT

Can we reserve these forty days for our LORD JESUS?
To imitate His Humanity on earth? The struggle, the
temptation, the reasoning power our LORD Has
gone through His argument with Satan;
Can we be that strong, too?
It started with the condemnation, the persecution, the
betrayal, the denial, the whipping, the lashes, the spitting,
the falling on the ground, with the heavy cross on His
Shoulder, the blood on His face freely flowing from
the deep pressure of the thorns on His head;
How much more can He take?
The shame He felt from the stripping of His
garment, the huge nails hammered on His
hands and feet, the insult of trying to quench His
thirst with the bile, vinegar taste on His mouth
standing tall without breath;
It didn't soothe the satisfaction of the sinners'
eyes, so a lance pierced deeply on His side
to make sure no signs of life seen.
Then he expired . . . excruciating pain felt in the
hearts of His beloved, His mother and relatives
witnessed the whole journey of His Passion.
The forty days remind us of our LORD's
redemptive sufferings
The forty days reassures us that salvation is at hand.
The forty days are given to us, for a chance to be
reunited with Him
So let us have our treasured moments to ponder
on His passion this season of Lent.
With or without forty days, let's keep our LORD's
love in our hearts forever.

THE DESIGNER'S MARK

I wish to erase and have a clean slate of the
marks of sinfulness
No amount of persuasion, to feel guiltless
and self-persecuted
The tender, soft hands of the Carpenter with
hollows through and through
The right side, in between the ribs, there's
a big scar, lanced by a faith-blinded centurion
The sash-like stripes from front to back
marked by hundreds of slash, whips and
with nauseating spits of the inhuman-men.

Now, the most beautiful face we've ever seen
was distorted by the excruciating facial pain,
with the red oozing fluid from the penetrated
thorny crown, pressed on His head.
We witness the agonizing scene of the Designer's
mark, yes the marks of our transgressions,
gracefully lifted by our LORD JESUS, the
Best Designer

Every Lent season we need to ponder on the characters who witnessed the Passion of our LORD JESUS CHRIST. Let us reconcile our thoughts from our hearts on how and why our LORD JESUS willingly did what He did, then ask ourselves, were we there?

WERE YOU THERE?

"Were you there?", a famous phrase known
for centuries
"Were you there?", a question asked by
the witnesses
"Were you there?" when the unforgettable
events happened?
Yes, were you there? May I ask and which
one were you?

John, the Beloved was there to support
JESUS' mother
He was deeply hurt, seeing his wounded Master
He cried so much with compassion and love
Yes, John was there, and there he was.

Who else was there at the foot of the cross?
A woman we know, a follower of JESUS
She is Mary of Magdala a well known sinner
whose life was transformed after her
JESUS' encounter.

There was another woman who approached
JESUS, she was on the way to Calvary, too
But she was there and wiped JESUS' meek face
and it marked on that white small cloth the
Image of our LORD . . . it was Veronica whose
name means the true Image of GOD.

Another character in uniform was there
known as the centurion
He witnessed the veil of the temple torn in the middle
He was stunned and uttered with conviction
"Truly this man was innocent and the Son of GOD."

Now, let's listen to the plea of the good thief, "Dismas"
He requested JESUS to remember him when he
come to His kingdom, and JESUS at once said,
"Today you will be with me in Paradise."

The most painful scene at the foot of the cross
was our Mother's broken heart and soul.
She could barely stand the agonizing pitiful
sight, of our LORD JESUS' torn flesh, wound
oozing fresh blood.
Our Mother was there and she never left from
Pilate's sentence of JESUS to death,
to the Calvary, cross-nailed and up high arm
stretched, pierced by lance on his side and up
to the last breath
Yes, she was there, how about you?
Did you wish you were there?

EASTER

The colorful flowers, the pastel colors
The beautiful hats, the Easter celebration
The eggs hunting, the Easter bunnies
The jelly beans, the Easter celebration
The basketful of candies, the children's
excitement, the chocolate bunny shapes
the Easter celebration, the church is full
but do we really know for sure
What we are celebrating this day?
Yes! It is the Resurrection of our LORD,
After His Agony and Passion.

EASTER SPRING

Easter Spring! Easter Spring!
Come and join me and let us sing
For today is the Day that the LORD
Has made
And let us rejoice and be glad in it.

Easter Spring! Easter Spring!
Revitalize of Spirit, renewal of heart
Come and let us celebrate our oneness
With CHRIST
Easter like Christmas, must always remain
In our hearts.

Enjoy the newness of life in our
Oneness with GOD
Happy Easter FOREVER!!!
Easter Spring! Easter Spring!

EASTER FOREVER

The Risen LORD is here with us today
To celebrate the Life, the Easter Sunday
The Life that has been renewed
After the wounds that we have caused.

Today is not only about the Resurrection
It is also about our LORD's retribution
Let us rejoice and sing for this celebration
To welcome in our hearts the great reconciliation.

Easter or not Easter, Good Friday or not
Let us always forgive from our hearts
Let us always rejoice and be renewed
And continue to have pleasant attitude.

So may our Easter celebration be a mark
Of changes
Changes from the good to the better
From the better to the best we can
Alleluia! To our Risen LORD, forever!

HALLOWEEN

"Trick or treat," the words that the kids utter on Halloween
Then go from house to house, rain or shine or any weather
Candies, chocolates, even cookies they put in their bags
Each of them wears horror costumes with awful looking masks.

Some parents accompany their kids in going around
to protect them from mean strangers and wild teens
Toddlers, preschoolers, young teens and adults
are indeed enjoying this Halloween thing.

Not only the children celebrates the Halloween
Adults too, and they even join a masquerade ball
Scary costumes they wear, with sophisticated masks
Are you one of them a Halloween freak?

The nice thing about Halloween
is the vast population of pumpkins
small ones, big ones you can see everywhere
with curved faces, candles lit at the center.

Nothing is wasted with those pumpkins
for in a few weeks time they will be pumpkin pies
they will be served together with the turkey,
corn bread and cranberry,
on another significant day, the "Thanksgiving Day."

So let us hurry up to finish this Halloween
So we can look forward for the Thanksgiving Day
No variations of costumes, but numerous thanking
for the Blessings and Graces, GOD Has given.
Thank You LORD for this celebration

THE HALLOW THAT WINS

Are you thankful only on Thanksgiving Day?
Are you grateful all the time?
Have you received intangible gifts in your life
Do you know the hallow that wins?

Saying "thank you" is a daily word used
Being grateful is one of the virtues
The gifts of the Holy Spirit are the best gifts
Now, that is the hallow that wins.

To hallow is to honor and be sacred
Not horror and be scared
To praise our LORD is one great grace
To cultivate virtues is a mile away to holiness
Being a virtuous person is a hallow that wins.

When we say the "Our Father," we uttered
"Hallowed Be Thy Name,"
When we ask help to pray, the Best Intercessor
is there
So let us pray all the time and ask our Blessed
Mother to intercede
for all our intentions we have indeed
Let us thank our LORD for the daily blessings
Not only on Thanksgiving Day but everyday.

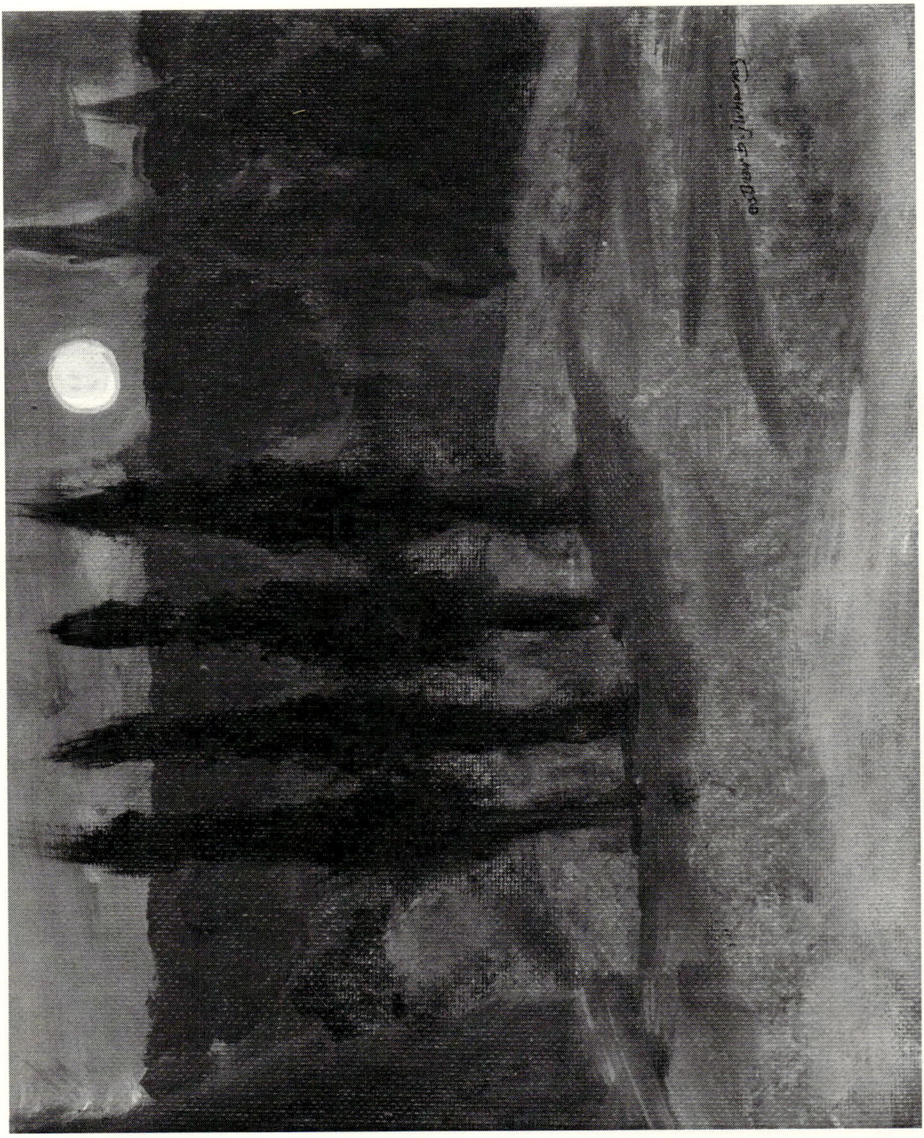

CHAPTER IV

PARABLES OF THE FABLES

The parables in the Bible give me an inspiration to write parables of my own. For me, writing short stories help me use more of my creativity. Some of the parables are based on my actual conversation with people and others from my watching television shows, and also from my keen observation of some animals' and pets' behavior. I can't help but to name this chapter "The Parables of Fables" because of its affinity. In my parables I utilized animals as the characters, that is to assimilate fables. Children are my favorites, too. They say that we learn from experiences and mistakes; I say, we learn from the kids, animals, especially our own pets. Where do you think we got our virtues? Did you say from the parables? Or from the fables? In the story of our creation, there are virtues and moral lessons learned. There was already a conversation between animal and the people. The serpent, the first animal (involved), played a big part of ruining a good relationship between GOD and the first couple. Adam was the one who gave names to animals, until Eve came and all the creatures joined the celebration of, "In The Beginning." We can think of a lot of virtues, lessons, parables and fables just by reading and knowing the very beginning of the Bible. Can you think of at least seven animals in Noah's Ark? Remember, GOD created everything in seven days and everything He created was good? Maybe we can create our own parables based on the first animals in the Bible. So let's flip the pages and visit the Animal Kingdom of moral lessons and virtues.

THE PARABLE OF WISDOM

In the land of the "The Dreamer,"
There is a dreamer roaming,
He is fascinated with the
Richness around him.
He is given the chance to pick
What he wants.
But there is a condition
That he must comply
He is to use it every time
And share to everyone
For if he fails to do it,
He is nothing but a real
"DREAMER."

THE PARABLE OF PATIENCE

Once upon a time, there was a tiny bird chirping
so loud that caught the attention of the other birds.
The other birds were watching this male bird
picking up with his tiny-tiny beak the pieces of
small scrap and debris, bringing them back and
forth from the ground up to the slender branch
of the tree.
He was doing this for the whole day.
He is like an artist, a sculptor building or molding
something and chirping continuously.
True enough, he built a sturdy beautiful nest for
his bird mate, soon to lay eggs.
Congratulations! Mr. Tiny Bird for your new family.

THE PARABLE OF HUMILITY

In the forest nearby there are two
trees talking
One is straight up and standing tall,
the other is short and full of leaves.
They look odd standing side by side
but they get along and always share
their ideas and opinions.
One day, the short tree asked the tall tree,
"Why is it that you can bend as low as you can?"
"Aren't you hurt reaching the ground?"
The tall tree responded, "Yes, it hurts,
but reaching the ground makes me feel
good, bowing down makes me talk to you
better, bending lower I can see you clearer,
and doing all of these makes me bigger
inside me.
Why can't we be like the tall tree, the
role model of humility.

THE PARABLE OF INNOCENCE

There was a young boy of fifteen,
very neat and good-looking and the only
boy among the offsprings.
The three sisters he has, are very
smart and intelligent.
Sometimes he feels bad, thinking
he is not smart.
But he always tries to do good in class.
One day he didn't go to school for
not feeling well.
His father brought him to the dentist
for gum pain.
The dentist confirms the tooth growth
in progress and he is starting to have,
"wisdom tooth" as the layman's term.
Upon knowing there is a wisdom tooth
growing, the young boy jumps with
joy, yelling and happily telling his
sisters that finally he can be smart and
pretty soon will have a wisdom to use.
Now, do you sometimes wish to be a
child again? I do.

THE PARABLE OF NATURE
(The Message Of A Blind Boy)

There is a boy who is blind since birth
He grows up with no playmates
He learns to communicate with the
birds and the trees.
Everyday of his life, he smiles with
delight in his heart.
While he's growing up he's studying
his surroundings,
He learns to count with the pebbles
in the stream.
He learns the alphabet with the fruits
on the trees.
He appreciates the sounds of the wind.
And here is the poem he speaks from his
heart and sees in his mind.

The wind I feel in my hand, my hair
blows as I ran.
The trees, big and small up standing,
welcoming the sun.
The sun flickers as the leaves move.
Its radiance challenges the eyes of
the onlookers.
The mountain curvatures balance,
from the top downward is a, view of a
portion of a land, and the overlooking
GOD's creation . . . "ME," the blessed blind.

THE PARABLE OF VICTORY

This is a story of a turtle and a rabbit
who always compete with each other;
Running a race is the game they play
Guess who won this simple game?

"Slow but sure," is the turtle's motto
Patience he has and its one of his virtues
The rabbit on the other hand is witty
and cunning
Always too confident, thinking
he would win.

So he took his time, to the extent
of dozing off under the tree
But he overslept, then the turtle passed
him-by, still walking briskly
until he reached the finish line
He won with the trophy in his hand.

In our lives we need the virtue of patience
We need to take matters one day at a time
We need to weigh things and not rush
Like the way the turtle moves and acts.
Can you do the same, slowly but surely?

Victory is not attained by intimidation nor under-estimation, but self-confident and determination.

THE PARABLE OF PERSISTENCE
(The Endless Story)

In the land of Ant-E-Bulum
There was a king named, "Zilon,"
He sent a messenger to the city, to
announce a contest to the community.

The contest is about the future
groom to be, for his daughter,
a princess, who is so pretty.
The king is looking for anyone,
rich or poor, who can tell an
"Endless Story."

Many gentlemen and guys came
from different places
just to tell a story without end.
But no one is successful to win
except for one, a humble peasant,
and he started his own parable.

"Once upon a time, there was a king
who was looking for someone who
could count the grains of rice in
his kingdom.
And there was a small "ant" who
bravely applied.
He started carrying one grain of rice
to the empty barn, from a huge
warehouse and started to count;
So he kept doing this back and forth,

*But he needed help to count and
requested the readers to join.
The warehouse has seven million
sacks of rice, so my dear readers
start counting now,
One grain to the barn, back to the
warehouse, two to the barn back to
the warehouse, three to the barn,
back to the warehouse . . .
Continue counting my avid readers,
while I marry the lady princess
in this town, are we done yet?*

PERSISTENCE HAS A REWARD.

THE PARABLE OF HOPE

I love turtles and have few turtles of my own. I see a lot of virtues in them. I always observed their witty, behaviors, especially "PONG", my favorite one. One of the virtues I witnessed is "hope."

An old turtle who lives in a cave
came out one day
He walks, he looks around, he listens
and smells his surroundings
He talks to himself and with a smile
he says, "O how beautiful this earth is!"
He enjoys the snow in the Winter
He likes the scent of the flowers
in the Spring
He basks the whole Summer
And in the Fall, he plays with the
fallen leaves.
He is there in the cave to contemplate
the beauty of everything that
GOD Has created.
What makes him live that long?
How heavy is the shell he carries along?
Why is he known as a slow creature?
The secret answer to these questions
Is his "hope to live for the beauty of life,"
And the "hope to carry on."
(In patience there is hope, in hope there is reward)

THE PARABLE OF OBEDIENCE

There is a widow with twin daughters
Both in their high school teens
One is good in literature and art
The other is good in science and math
These twins are very studious
They always excel in every class
They have perfect attendance
They are always prepared in any exam
One day their mother asked one of them
to do the laundry and to the other to
clean the pantry
They are engrossed with their studying
and ignored what their mother is saying
What good it is to be intelligent and with
excellent grades, if you can't even show
some kind of obedience?

The key to a better Christian is to be obedient.
Come to think of it . . . because of our Blessed
Mother's obedience, we have JESUS
in our lives.

THE PARABLE OF PRAYER

Two little kids are in the playground
talking to each other
One is a little boy and the other is
a little girl
The girl asked the boy if he could
sing a song
The boy gladly replied, "Yes, I can,
do you want to hear?"
The girl nodded.
"Jack and Jill went up the hill,
to ask our GOD the Father,
Jack knelt down and bowed his head
to thank the LORD for his sweater."
After that, Jill clasped her hands
and closed her eyes and asked GOD
to look after her kitten.
So both kids smiled and cheerfully
part ways, leaving the beauty and
wonder of prayers in their hearts,
forever, Amen!

THE PARABLE OF GRATITUDE

A group of turkey gathered around the table
The head turkey made a short speech
The question he asked with gobble-gobble
"Aren't you proud we have something
to share?"
Without us, Thanksgiving Day is not complete
Like without GOD, the human beings are incomplete.
So my dear turkey friends, let us take turns
Gobble-gobble, Happy Thanksgiving Day
To all, turkeys included!

THE PARABLE OF COMMITMENT

A young turtle walks slowly and meets an older
turtle on the way to the airport. He asks the older
turtle what the time is, because he needs to be at the
airport that evening to pick-up another young fellow
turtle. Imagine the number of hours he must walk.
It's quite a distance and it's no joke.
He starts walking in the morning to give ample time
for his(being) slow nature reptile friend.
So, do you have this kind of virtue?
How committed are you to the things you do?

Esther B. Jimenez

THE PARABLE OF JUSTICE

There is a newly- wed deer in the jungle
The husband requested the wife to
prepare a meal
He has a taste for a fish and went to
the lake near-by
He didn't know how to swim, so fishing
he did try
While he was about to throw the rod
with the hook on a string
he saw two dolphins in the still motor boat
Fighting, grabbing the huge fish
So he approached them and said,
"Stop fighting here's what you can do."
"You take the head," and to the other
he said, "You take the tail and the middle
give it to the judge."(the judge is the deer)
Now everyone has a share and I don't
need to stay longer, and my wife has
something to cook now and prepare for
our dinner, fair enough?

THE PARABLE OF WONDERS

A group of ants gather in a small cave
to talk about the problem they have
The problem is that, they would be
soon evicted out of the molehill they built.

This group of ants start to move out
each carries a piece of crumbs in
their mouth
Every time they cross ways, they
whisper or maybe kiss each other.
Have you ever thought what they're
talking about?

Does it mean affection and compassion?
Does it mean a warning of upcoming
danger?
Or is it a ritual that they practice?
Or is it one of GOD's wonder of wonders?
Yes, it is, so don't wonder why?

THE PARABLE OF ABUNDANCE

In a small village there's a couple with
a dozen kid
They hardly could cope with the daily needs
The family is so happy being together
They always pray before each meal.

The family receives donation once in a while.
Mind you, they are very grateful for
that chance
The children are polite and respectful
and you won't hear them complain at all.

Abundance for them is not of materials
but the riches of their relationship
Abundance is a nourishment not only
of the food, but of the soul.

So, will you still dwell on your
complaints and grumbles?
Be thankful all the time, that is Abundance.

THE PARABLE OF FAITH

The invincible truth is what it is
"Prove it to me," is what it takes
"To see is to believe," is the challenge
Don't you know that faith is within
yourself?

This is the story of a Doubtful Mind
who always question things around
always curious and wanders all the time
This mind has no peace, so the heart
interferes
The heart speaks so proudly
without tinge of doubt.
It tells the mind to be silent;
      to be sensitive with the surroundings
      to just ponder on the wonderful things
      to listen and feel the Presence of the
      One who creates everything.
Do you have a faith as little as the
mustard seed?

THE PARABLE OF GENEROSITY

A young millionaire once attended an auction
He looked around and checked his competition
He saw at least seven very rich people
And in his mind he knows he can beat them.
The young millionaire is so aggressive and
bid so high, not even noticing an old man
raising his hand
The old man stood up and said, "I am the owner
of the land and I changed my mind,"
"I don't want this item be auctioned."
This item in auction is a piece of land.
He rather gives it to the family man.
This family man was patiently waiting
for whomever won, because he would
ask for a job back in the farm.
He was the farmer who used to take care
of the said land.
The old man gladly handed to the family man
the title of the land.
And in his heart he knows this is a gift
of a lifetime.
Do we have a heart like that old millionaire man?

THE PARABLE OF TRUTH

Two men were walking along the street
One man is an engineer
The other is a defending lawyer
The engineer asked the lawyer if he
ever told the truth in his life
The lawyer just commented
"Telling the truth is my job."
The conversation continued and when
they were about to cross the street
the lawyer remembered that he must be
in court to defend a client.
A question was asked again by this engineer
"What if the client indeed killed someone?"
"Can you prove that he is innocent?"
The lawyer confidently claimed,
The truth is, I have never lost a case."
Inside the court the engineer was there.
He is the client to be prosecuted.
Question? Is the lawyer telling the truth,
that he never loses a case?
Is the engineer guilty? Or innocent?
Remember, the "truth will set you free."

THE PARABLE OF FORGIVENESS

There is a king who is so cruel
He always has somebody to
blame everyday
He curses and punishes the captives
He never listens to the plea of others.
One day he got ill and worried too much
He called the best doctor in town
The doctor was so honest and told him this,
"Your case is terminal and no remedies."
"But if you start forgiving yourself,
A chance of recovery is at hand."
The king started to wonder how and
when to begin.
The doctor then again told him,
"You have seventy times seven to
forgive and be forgiven, but start now
from within yourself."
From then on the king got better
Joy in his face is always seen
He didn't realize that it only takes
to count this "forgiving game,"
From seventy times down.
(Read between the lines)

THE PARABLE OF GRIEF

A herd of elephants were running
in the jungle
They were being chased by the poachers.
The ground was shaken with the
pounding steps of the herds.
The parent elephants were trying to
protect the young ones by placing
the young ones between them.
Unfortunately, there were at least
three young ones hurt and killed.
Since they were only at their youth
and the tusks are not sellable yet,
the poachers left.
The herds grouped together at night
and they were creating trumpet
sound-like cry, and was heard all over
the jungle, sounds of hurting elephants,
sounds of lamentation.
People that were there witnessed the
pouring of the herds' tears.
Do they have emotions? Yes.
Are they grieving, certainly yes.

THE PARABLE OF SIMPLICITY

In the garden by the river there was a lady picking-up the beautiful flowers from her garden. Then all of a sudden she ran across a man with long white beard. The man was amazed seeing those beautiful flowers, and to his amazement he asked the lady, "What is your secret having blooming garden?"
"Sir," replied by the lady, "First of all, there's no secret." "I just think of how GOD created the first garden named, "Eden."
I just simply water them, trim and talk to my garden, (the flowers and the plants,) no extra attention, no fertilizer, nor any chemicals, then they bloom themselves.
I am enjoying everyday just seeing their beauty."

THE PARABLE OF DISCIPLINE

"Good health habit is a good example of self-discipline." the hare teacher is telling the young hare pupils.
She was telling them the importance of eating fresh fruits and essence of proper sleep.
One of the things she emphasized was, the proper hand washing and the brushing of their two front teeth every morning, night and sometimes after meals.
The hare pupils are very compliant and have self-discipline. The young hares have been practicing health habits as evidenced of having beautiful strong teeth. So, "Bunny with good health habits, "are one disciplined rabbits."

THE PARABLE OF LEADERSHIP

A flock of mallard zoomed up and flew up to attend a large group meeting near-by huge, man-made lake. There were other flocks attended from different places of the city. The theme of the meeting is about grouping together and to find out the places they would be assigned as in "territorial assignments."
They have agreed to group themselves from seven to ten birds in a group. They also agreed to have a leader in each group, to guide them and be responsible for them. The flocks have their own assigned dwelling places. So after the meeting they flew back to their old places and some to their new place. They flew up with a leader in each group, forming a V-shape, with seven to ten mallards following their leaders. So when you see mallards flying in V-shape it is because they are following their leaders. What a role model for a leadership and come to think of it, the V, might stand for victory.

I didn't realize that I have already written something about the elephant herds in this chapter, The Parable of the Fables; With a few months apart, I still have in my heart how the elephants handle their grief. I have read this information and I couldn't erase it from my mind, the natural compassion that this creature is displaying. Grief and suffering has the same level of emotion and these two parables have a great impact in people's lives.

THE PARABLE OF SUFFERING

Grief is an unpleasant feeling and it is one of the most hurting feelings one can ever imagine.
A group of elephant herd formed a circle to pour out their pains and hurt for the loss of the two baby elephants, who were shot by the poachers. The bodies of the young ones were at the middle of the circle and the elephants chant and moan and heard throughout the jungle.
The mother elephant (consider their leader) called for a meeting. This is a group pf matriarch dynasty, in which the mother elephant has the say so. She announced to the herds that they need to double their effort to hide and be alert for the poachers, because they couldn't afford to lose more young ones. It pained them so much seeing them killed. The mother elephant emphasized the importance of being vigilant, watching each other's back.
Can you imagine a huge mammal with soft, sensitive and selfless heart?
Suffering is not only felt by human heart, other creatures too like elephants.

THE PARABLE OF LAUGHTER

They say that, "Laughter is the best medicine."
What if the laughter is the one causing the pain?
There is this big yellow bumble bee buzzing around the shrubs and circling the hibiscus flowers, sipping the nectars. All of a sudden someone shouted as if stung by a bee. True enough, a middle-aged gardener was stung by the yellow bumble bee. The buzzing sound became louder to get the attention of the passers-by.
If there is such "laugh out loud", there is also, "buzz out loud." Did you ever think that when a bee stung you, he is very happy he did it? Have you also thought that bees' laugh might be their defense for not being recognized?
So, instead of avoiding the bees, be friendly with them and see if he can buzz out loud, ha! ha! ha! Laugh out loud . . . life is too short!

THE PARABLE OF COMMON SENSE

A giraffe and a monkey went out for a date. They had breakfast at the near-by coffee house.

After ordering their breakfast, the monkey went to the counter to get hot water for her tea, (from the thermos.) Since, she is not that tall, the hot water splatters on her face. So both of them went to the manager to suggest to move the thermos with hot water to where the coffee thermos are. The manager didn't pay attention to their complaint/suggestion, so they put it in writing and they drop it in the suggestion box.

After few months, the giraffe and the monkey went for a breakfast date again in the same coffeehouse. Guess what? The thermos with hot water is already in lined with the other coffee thermos.

Now every short adult can reach the thermos with hot water. We have two satisfied customers. Is it true that customer is always right?

THE PARABLE OF INDUSTRIOUSNESS

A spider couple was having a one on one talk after their dinner. The spider wife was pregnant and they were discussing where to settle down, since the place where they were at that time was demolished. The area had been swept clean.
So the spider husband started looking for a little bit dark area, with dirty corners or possibly with trees around. Luckily, he found one and he started weaving, webbing up and down, side to side and as if he was doing this "bungee- jumping." He was also working like a construction worker in a contractual project,(working double time.)
He really built a sturdy house for his wife and the future spider lings. Every spider in the town admire him, and he became the model of fatherhood.
We can be industrious too, if we want too, right fellow readers?
I know a lot of people are scared of spiders. Let us just be gentle and don't kill them. They might kill the bugs that would bite you tomorrow.

THE PARABLE OF SELF-CONTROL

Somewhere in Thailand there is this School of Elephants. There is this elephant teacher who teaches elephant math. So the herd is learning the basic counting of 1,2, 3 numbers.
One day an elephant student approached the teacher and poured out his problem. It's not about math lesson, but about his temper at home. He is always in trouble even with his playmates.
"Teacher," the student asked, "What shall I do to control my temper?"
"Well," the teacher answered, "Now that you learned to count numbers, it would help you with your problem." And she added, "If you feel like you are losing your temper or can't control your anger, count from 1 to 20 slowly and before you reach the 20, you'll calm down."
Well folks, instead of 1-10 as the saying goes, the teacher says 1 to 20, why? Because the elephants are big. You don't want to encounter this elephant with temper, do you?

THE PARABLE OF KINDNESS

One Sunday, the animals in the jungle were celebrating the freedom day. In their minds, they were thinking, of "No Poachers" on Sunday, so it's a day to celebrate. In the middle of their fellowship, they heard shots at the near distance. So everyone ran as fast as they can. Most of the animals were able to hide, but there was this monkey trapped at the edge of the cliff. He was trying to cross to the other cliff, but he couldn't. Unfortunately, there were no trees around for him to swing. A giraffe saw his struggle, so he extended his long neck from one cliff to the other and the monkey then crossed between the cliffs and used the giraffe as the bridge.
Now, everyone is safe. Is this kindness or what? How many are there of this kind nowadays . . . (the giraffe's sympathetic nature?)

THE PARABLE OF COURAGE

There is a place in Wisconsin where you could see bald eagles just hanging out in harmless surrounding near a barn.

One young eagle got fractured while trying to practice his flying stunt. He was practicing because he would like to join the flying exhibition in the near-by town. His mother tried to do the emergency application of sling and bandage. But his heart pulls him down, not interested in going back to his practice. He didn't even want to fly at low level. The bald eagle is manifesting "eagle depression".

And because of the wound and fracture that he attained, he thought of the worse thing . . . that the accident might happen again. The bald eagle mother told him a story of a successful bald eagle who won the most precious award of very long years ago. That bald eagle became the national bird symbol of America.

Now folks, did you really know the symbol of this beautiful bird? The symbolism of this bald eagle is strength and freedom, but I have to add, "courage."

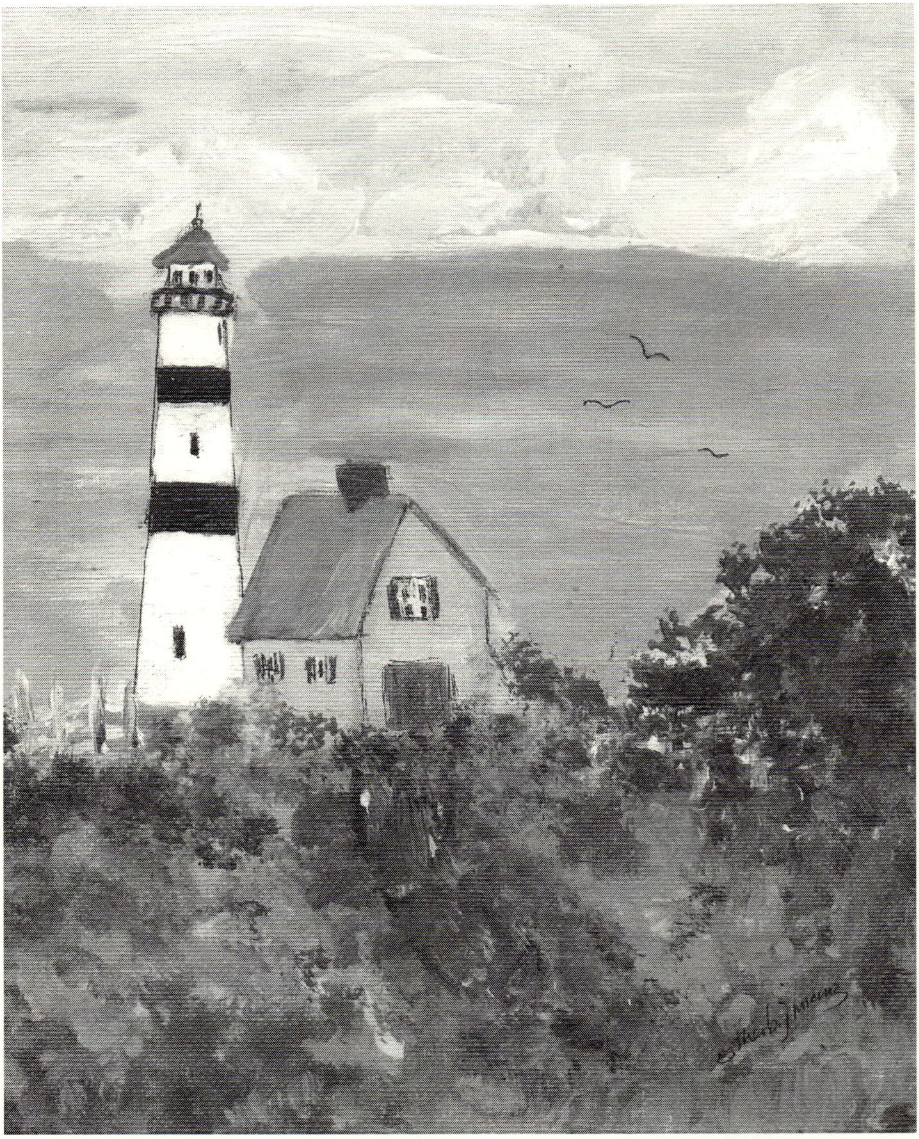

CHAPTER V

FRIENDSHIP

An author once said, "Community is essential to us as human beings. We know how important it is to have friends." Friends could be your father, mother, brother, sister, cousin, companions and relatives. They are blessings that bring warmth and happiness into our lives. They share our joy and help us endure our sufferings. This chapter is about friendship relationship.

Here's a common question, what is friendship? I have my own definition of friendship. For me, friendship is a ship loaded with friends, sailing together, balancing their movements through rhythmic paddling so that no one will sink. That's what friends should do, to treat each other fairly, to support one another and to nurture each souls, so that you'll have smooth relationship. You might have your our own definition of friendship, as you might have your own concept of love. Whatever you have, make sure to treasure the friendship forever. You can have one hundred friends right now, but you can't have a high five best friend. Now, let's find out who are our friends and who we are with them. Happy friendship sailing!

THE PRECIOUS GIFT, THE FRIENDSHIP

I am blessed with what I have
I am proud to tell the world
I am pleased to claim my treasure
I am an owner of a gift called friendship.

I found a friend that I can trust
I found a friend that I can call (anytime)
I found a friend that cares
I found a precious gift called friendship.

I thought I would never find a friend that
I'll treasure
Now I am glad to have a genuine one for sure
I am confident that my secret is safe
Because I have this precious gift called friendship.

I thank GOD for the gift of friendship
I thank the Holy Spirit for guiding us
I thank our Blessed Mother for her love
And I thank my friend for being my
Precious gift.

WHAT IT MEANS TO BE A TRUE FRIEND?

A true friend is someone you can trust
Someone you can freely say what you want
A true friend is willing to listen
Whether it is a complaint or just plain sharing
A true friend is there all the time
In times of low and high moments
A true friend is honest and frank
Will approach you with sincerity of heart
A true friend is thoughtful and mindful
of your needs and makes effort to help
A true friend will defend you and not
ridicule you in front of anybody
A true friend knows when you're sad
and when you're upbeat and glad
A true friend can keep secret no matter what
through thick and thin, till death do they part
A true friend is truly a best friend to keep.

IN FRIENDSHIP

You open your lips and your heart
To tell someone about your life
This is the start of your bonding
And it is called, "friendship."
Willingness to be part of each other,
And it's an awe
Trial and error is part of the game
And you encounter this during the bonding
Feelings might get hurt, but does it matter?
As long as you know that your friend
is there
Indeed it's true, it's hard to find a friend
who is loyal
You have to accept each other's
differences and that's real friendship
You're lucky if you have one, if you don't,
find one now
In friendship, you should be willing
to listen and have shoulders to lean on
A warm embrace and hug tight must be
freely given without any question.
One thing you should know in friendship is,
there is something in common in the
spirit flow . . . that JESUS CHRIST is in
between their friendship
He is the True Friend that brought them
together and always there.
You are never alone in this world
because you have our LORD waiting
for our friendship with Him.
If you want to know what a real friend is,
read the Scriptures for more virtues
Virtues are weapons for choosing a true
friend and friendship with GOD is the
strongest and lasting one.

A FRIEND

A friend to me is . . . someone you can turn to
A friend to me is . . . a person stands by me all
   the way through
A friend to me is . . . a friend like you who is
   always there come what may
A friend to me is . . . somebody who is loyal
   and honest
A friend to me is . . . a fellow who cares for
   me, in spite of my shortcomings
A friend to me is . . . a pal who is so understanding
A friend to me indeed is a friend like you period.
Yes, my friend, may I say you're the best.
A friend is indeed difficult to find if
you're searching for a genuine one.
So let's treasure the friends we have now
And keep that strong friendship in our hearts.
The friend that I have is you . . . and I thank
GOD for having you
That's what a friend to me, through
thick and thin, rain or shine, or come what may.

The following poem was written in 1971 for, a used to be a best friend. This is one of my first few poems. Time changed, things changed, life changed but the way I treasure my friends would never change. I always thank our LORD for the gift of friendship.

"YOU"

What makes you, makes me love you
How many times I was hurt
Still no space for regrets
You, who brought happiness in my life
And you who at times makes me suffer
Suffering, longing for you to be mine forever.
I miss you and your being
I don't want to miss saying I love you
I don't want to lose you
But your being you, makes me decide
To leave you
I wish I could love you, because
of who you are
And I have to accept the truth that
You are you
Needless to say, I am but me, too
And may you just be yourself
And may yourself and your being
Have a good life!

PROMISES FROM A FRIEND

Do you believe in saying, "Promises
Are made to be broken?"
Though promises are made to be
broken, I say they are solutions
and consolations in life too
Promises can change ones character
When you're hurt, you'll hear a
promise, and as soon ar you hear
that, you are relieved and pacified
Promises, I'll say, too, serve as . . .
Inspiration
Challenge
Relief
To us.
Shall we say, give the person another chance?

THE BOOK OF FRIENDSHIP

I've read a book about friendship
It gives me an insight as always is
It tells about my own experience
It reveals oneself without knowing it.
Famous poets write their own concept
of friendship, from their hearts they speak
They share their experience about their
friends, the loyalty, the betrayal and the
long lasting friendship.
You can be an author of a book
You can tell from cover to cover your
experiences about your friends
the seasonal ones and the friend
for a reason and a friend you can
claim your own
Start now your book of friendship
share, learn and be proud of it;
Treasure your friends, treasure that
Book of friendship
Keep it in the safe library, where the
center of your heart is
Let's be thankful and grateful
for the greatest and Best Friend of all
The Real author of the Book of Friendship
The Author of our life, our Creator.

FRIENDLY ADVICE

You said it just happened, it didn't just happen
You made it happen
You said you know what you're doing
But you know what you're doing is wrong
You said you're struggling
But you don't want to stop
You said you will try your best
But your best is not enough
You said you will stop, but you don't
Want to give effort
You said to leave you alone
But we are only after your soul.
You said your kids will be okay in the long run
The longer it takes, the ruin takes place.
You said you're thinking
You're not thinking from the heart
You're thinking from the flesh
Life is too short, my friend
Don't waste your investment
It's never too late, because
Heaven can wait
But you have to do two things
Ask for forgiveness and repent.

FRIENDSHIP . . . IT IS

A friend like you is worth to keep
You are genuine, so precious to have
Just be the same anytime, anywhere
My friend, I say you're the best.
One thing I want you to know is
I am here for you, all the way through
I am just a phone call away, my friend
My heart is open and willing to listen
Truly, your friendship is important to me
I pray to GOD for its authenticity
The bonding we have, the feelings we shared
I praised GOD for this wonderful gift,
"The Friendship."

THE FRIENDSHIP PRAYER

O LORD, I thank You for the friends I have
I thank You for the time we spent
I thank You for the tears and laughter
That we always share at any time moments.
Allow me LORD to extend my help
for my friends near or far
Allow me to just be a good listener
And to just have a warm embrace
Grant us the gift of compassion in
times of adversity.
I pray for the gift of friends O LORD
for teaching me to be a friend to all
All that I pray for friendship LORD
I pray in Your Holy Name, Amen!

The indifference happens when groups are in the verge of splitting or any division or segregation. We tried to be civilized sometimes and if can't be, major feud results. So, why the indifference?

THE INDIFFERENCE

The closeness is gone
The caring diminished
The smiles are limited
Why the indifference?

Where is the sisterhood?
Where is the warmth?
Where is the love?
Why the indifference?

We say, "Let's stand together"
We say, "We love each other"
We say, "We are in unity with
CHRIST."
Why the indifference?

The indifference will surface
After the division
But are we going to tolerate
This unpleasant scene?
Let us be together in hearts
Let us respect each other
Let us go on with our missions
And forget the indifference
My sisters, my friends, let's have
Fellowship in mind, heart and soul.

ARE YOU LOOKING FOR A FRIEND?

A true friend offers unconditional love
A sincere friend will tell you when you're wrong
A generous friend is willing to listen
An honest friend is open
A faithful friend fulfills a promise
A loyal friend gives regards to your feelings
A thoughtful friend thinks of your welfare
A trustful friend can keep secrets
A sweet warm friend verbalizes her concern
for a friend.
A compassionate friend knows how to
hug and embrace.
A new friend must know the virtues of friendship
An old friend knows how to maintain friendship.
A true friendship is a mission ready, avails
oneself in time of emergency.

LAUGHTER . . . A FRIEND SHOULD POSSESS

They say that, "laughter is the best medicine"
I say, "laughter is a gift that we should
practice more often;"
I love to be with the person who has a great
sense of humor
I love to share my own laughing moments
I enjoy the short moments of laughter and jokes.

A BEST FRIEND

How do you define a Best Friend?

A best friend is someone you have
spent a quality time with.
A best friend is someone you can
lean on in times of adversity.
A best friend is someone you can
share your deepest secret.
A best friend is someone who
is not judgmental.
A best friend is someone you can
walk with, to appreciate nature.
A best friend is someone you can
dine with and talk non-sense.
A best friend is someone who can
share tears and laughter
A best friend is someone you can
depend on in any situation.
A best friend is someone who
believes and trusts in your friendship.
A best friend is someone who can confront
you, if you're 're doing something wrong,
and can correct you with diplomacy.
A best friend is not just a friend, she/he
is someone you can keep forever.
A best friend is CHRIST centered and
believes in moral values.
If you are this type of "best friend",
then look for someone like you.
May your friendship be the best
of friendship.

This is one of my exciting feelings in my life . . . a surprise call from my ex-best friend., a very unforgettable friend of more than three decades ago. Sad to say but we didn't have a pleasant closure, yet it didn't matter, as long as the second closure is very civil and yes very pleasant. She called me to thank me of receiving a book that I wrote, "Bible Tidbits" and claimed she enjoyed reading it. I will make sure you will receive a copy of this book, Vicky B. This poem is for you.

A SURPRISE CALL

The phone rang and the voice said,
"It's Vicky," and she said her last name.
I didn't believe it was my friend of
years ago, didn't recognize her voice,
and I got no clue?
But when I asked her, what my middle
name is, (just to check), but with no
seconds wasted, she did remember.
This is indeed a surprise call and it
made my day.
A surprise call that made me ponder again.
A surprise call that brought joy and delight
in my thoughts and in my heart.
Yes, a surprise call that I'll treasure
in my life forever.
I love you my friend indeed, it's real.
I just want you to know how I feel
The peace in my heart I finally attained,
hearing your voice again.
It's me, you and GOD who witnessed
the genuine friendship we had and
continue to have.
Again, thank you for the surprise call.
Thank You GOD for loving us all.

This poem was written before our class reunion. I gave this poem (with a frame) on October, 1995.

I HONOR YOU, MY FRIEND CHING

I have a friend named, "Ching", my classmate
in School of Nursing
She is not an ordinary person, she is special,
she is my best friend.
As I recalled during my school days we had
some fun and joy together
We were on the same vibes
and our personalities clicked on the spot
We speak our own language
and we do communicate well
We understand what's in our hearts
even though we are apart.
Just imagine the years that passed-by
almost thirty-five years on the count
Until now we are strongly connected
because we are spiritually bonded
We still keep in touch by short notes or cards
And for longer chit-chat, catching-up,
the phones are there for us
I would like to honor you, Ching,
my bosom friend
for a lot of reason and here they are:
"You are witty, cute and jolly,"
"You have a sense of humor and you're funny,"
"You are a caring person and a devoted nurse,"

"You are a generous and thoughtful gal,"
"You are conscientious and always are concerned,
About the people you loved and care most of all,"
"You are brave and courageous woman,"
"You are tenacious, smart and loving lady,"
"And an understanding, compassion and loyal person,"
What more can I say, you're everything a friend can own.
I honor you my friend, most of all, for being you
And because GOD loves you and in His Image,
He created you.
"I LOVE YOU AND I MISS YOU, MY FRIEND"

MY PRECIOUS FRIEND CHING

C- ompassionate woman, caring and courageous
H- umble, in every word she says
I- nsightful, inspiring, I really love this lady
N- o dull moments in our conversation, she's full of life
G- racious in her words, gentle in her actions

B- rave heart she has, bold in every step she makes

L- oving, one of the best qualities she possesses
A- ccommodating, approachable, with welcoming hands
Z- ealous, she became and now her faith zooms
O- bedient, not only to friends' advices, but to GOD's will.

CHING B. LAZO, you're an angel to everyone!

TREASURED MOMENTS

Memories to ponder, sadness and laughter
Precious moments, treasured ones
Togetherness, aloneness, shared with quality
I can only recall
I can only smile
I can only share the treasured moments
The value of friendship is tested through
The quality of treasured moments
To you my friend I offer my sincerity
And loyalty
To you my confidant, I reveal my
True identity
To the most understanding and
Accommodating fellow, these messages
From my heart I relay to none other
Than my precious and treasured friend,
Ching B. Lazo . . . I love you!

MY FRIEND, ONE OF A KIND

I long to hear your voice my friend
I miss our conversation on the phone
I look forward to share with you
How my days go and yours, too.
I called you many times, but I hear no reply
I wonder and asked my self why?
Then I realized maybe you need your
moments of silence.
Maybe you are in pain, that is how much
I care, not to demand an answer.
I try to understand how you're
dealing with your cancer.
My friend, it's okay to not lift up the phone
I just want to let you know I respect
your silence.
And anytime you want to share, I'm just
a phone call away
One time while I was driving, I dialed
your number
I missed you so much that moment,
I wanted to hear your voice
and I need to know if I can help ease
your pain
After few days you returned my call
But you only left a message
Because I was in the conference

And I felt sad and weak
I wished I had my cell phone turn on
Today is a very significant day for me
September 07,2005 nine at night
I hear your voice again on the other line.
We talk, we laugh and we cry
O my friend, I miss you so much
I could feel your breath sound
I know you are suffering in pain
I mention to you my plan to go to California
and we agreed to see each other on October.
Yes my friend I now can sleep soundly
Now that I hear from you again
I love you so dearly, my one of a kind friend.

I WISH I COULD

I wish I could share with you my thoughts
about how I would deal with the situation
where you are right now.
I would spend my time appreciating the
nature, the creatures and creations of GOD
on earth.
I would show my love to everyone in my
family and in the circle of friends, even
to the new people I meet, the strangers as
well, and be reconciled with the people who
have hurt me and people I've hurt.
I would take time to walk and smell the
fragrance of the flowers including the
blossoms of the lemon and orange trees.
I would call my friends that I haven't
heard for so long.
I would learn to be detached with the things
I was comfortable with, meaning to get out
of my comfort zone.
I would donate my used clothes and some
material things to the needy people,
or to my relatives that can take care of the
treasured valuables.
I would hug and embrace every chance
I have, my mother, father, sister, brothers,
nephews, nieces, in-laws, grandkids and all
my loved ones.
I would let them know that I love them, by
uttering the words, "I love you."

I would maybe do some volunteer jobs in the
hospital or anywhere that needed my service.
I would enjoy my precious moments left in
this world, by communicating with GOD
and would have asked GOD's grace to do
His will, and would have asked the Holy Spirit
to guide me every step of the way.
I would imitate JESUS in the humblest way
and ask for His mercy everyday.
I would beg for our Blessed Mother ever
Virgin for her intercession for my journey
to heaven.
Yes, I would ask for my real home, the Eternal
Kingdom, my final destination.
My friend, I would like to share with you
my love and deepest thoughts of my desire
to see face to face our Almighty.
Again, I wish and pray for the right time to
let you know about my wishes.
When you and I are ready, GOD will let us
know; I wish my wishes come true.

MY MESSAGE TO YOU, IN YOUR GRAVE

I wonder what it feels inside the dark space?
Without the moist on the glass near your face?
Lying on a fitted bed, elegantly dressed
not hearing any of my message.

My friend, why did you stop being a friend?
What made you think our friendship was gone?
How could you be silent that long,
when you could still share your feelings?

You knew I was aware of your sufferings and pain
You knew how much I cared for you and your welfare
You knew that we had a good foundation of the
friendship that we have started
And you knew that I would be there any moment
I am needed.

I knew that your coldness started when I went to
visit you
I had only one reason why I wanted to see you
I just wanted to serve you even for a short time
but it seemed it was an unpleasant reunion.

You had good people around you that took care
Of your needs
But there was a tension that I felt when I was there
Was I a burden? Was I not welcomed? Was I a
threat? Or was I not your friend?

My friend, I have to ask you these questions, for I
want to have peace in my heart.
Many times, I called you, but you never replied
It was not like you, you were a jolly person,
a loving, thoughtful and caring fellow.

Why sudden changed? I asked for your
forgiveness a dozen times, even I knew I
didn't do anything that would make you mad
or upset with me. Again, why my friend?
If you wanted understanding on my part,
you knew I would give it to you
If you wanted to leave you alone, I tried to
fulfill that
If the people around you didn't want our
friendship, that . . . I could never understand.
If you wanted to leave this earth without
talking to me, again why?

Where was that promise of waving your hand
when you reached heaven?
Where was that assurance of watching me
when I feel low?
Where was the friend that I used to talk to
when she was feeling blue?
Where are you now, can you hear me through?

I was there one time and you showed me how
you have prepared for your final journey
from your fitted bed to the resting place
From the songs you wanted and the eulogy
You wanted me to speak
and from funny jokes you created
and the sweet good-byes you requested.

My friend, I know there is heaven and I know
we'll meet again someday, but I wished that
I have a way to send you my messages, my friend
I pray that in my moments of solitude, I could
feel you and pray that our LORD maybe with
you in your journey to His Kingdom.
Again please forgive me and I forgive you too.
I love you my friend and I still hope to see your
waving hand up there!

TO FORGIVE IS . . . TO LET GO

The hurt and pain that I feel
The heartaches that still linger
The sleepless nights are still there
All these feelings are indeed real.

I feel betrayed, it seems injustice
To just let the friendship ruined
By the miscommunication and silence
By undue influence of the people around.

I tried to cope with the unexpected news
I cried and shouted at the top of my voice
I was angry and full of hatred
For a while I was losing myself.

I was craving for the inner healing
I poured out my sentiments to GOD
I asked the help of the Holy Spirit
And our Mother Mary to intercede.

I am thankful for my sisters around
Who poured out their love and care
Their prayers, and warm embraces
Aided me in my utmost inner healing.

Thank You LORD, thank you my sisters
For the inner healing that I attained
For the gift of forgiveness and peace
And now I am letting go of my ill-feelings
And letting GOD to enter into my heart.

FOR YOU MY BELOVED FRIEND

I ponder the day we met
I treasure the memories we spent
I linger on the thoughts of being with you
Yes my beloved friend, I sincerely love you.

I care for you and want to serve you
I think of you every single day
I am fond of you, my beloved friend
I am here for you, flesh and blood.

The times that we are not together
The times that you're hurting are
The times I thought of reconciling
with you right away, my beloved friend.

So, my friend, these messages are for you
to let you know how much I love you
In my heart you are there and
in my thoughts, you'll be there forever.

My beloved friend, our friendship is
for us to keep, to be with each other
through thick and thin and to stand
for what we believe and that friendship
is GOD's gift and never have to be taken
for granted.
I pray for the blessings of our friendship,
in JESUS' friendship name, Amen!

BE AN ADVOCATE

A very good friend of mine
verbalizes her ill-feelings
physically stressed out
emotionally exhausted;
Question asked
Is GOD really here?
Right now? At this moment?
Why did He let me feel this way?
I listened, my feedback?
Yes my friend, our LORD is here
and is there! With you, listening
watching you: I understand
you're frustrated in your workplace.
Internalizing everything,
But you know what?
Try this, will you?
Talk to GOD again,
Surrender all your concerns
Submission is all He wants
Trust Him, have Faith
He'll guide you every step of the way
I'll pray for you, as I've promised.

SUBTLETY

I received a call from a friend, inviting me
to attend her birthday and she'll be fifty.
I don't want to lie, I don't want to attend,
I know that date I'll have a commitment
to do my volunteer job in the hospice.
She told me to not avail myself on the
volunteer thing, because it's only
once in a lifetime that she'll be in her
golden year;
But LORD, one of my changes in my
transformation is, to keep away from
any socialization
Not that I am proud of my change of
direction, not of hypocrisy, not of false
pretensions, but I just don't want to, LORD
I know LORD, You will understand
But will she? Will the rests of my friends do?
LORD, please lead me, Amen!

RELEASE

Things in my mind
Needs clarification
Questions that need answers
Shall I call you to find out?

You're a close friend
Trusted one, I say
I called you to seek the truth
Still nothing happened.

I called you again, with courage
To ask
Why you hurt me that much?
The truth I heard from your lips
No need to argue, peace we both want
Forgiveness, I grant

At least it gives me a relief
A release of emotion I did
A healthy confrontation I urged
A holy release is indeed helpful.

You apologized and so did I
Patch-up things make amends
Forgiveness happened, felt better
Release! Release! Release!
The truth sets me free.

REFLECTION OF COURAGE

In times of distress, in times of stress
We feel helpless, we feel the weakness
The strength that we need, we are on
to search
The awareness of Someone remains
All we need is to reach out and call for
the Sovereign One, need not to shout
Who else, but our Creator, the All Might
Who can and will give the courage we want
GOD grants courage for those who seeks
Me and my friend ask for it
She and I are spiritually connected
Because we have the reflection of courage.

IN TIME OF NEED

In time of need, you can tell who your friends are
In time of need, support of a group is there
In time of need, your folks are around you
In time of need, genuine relationship is transparent
In time of need, big ears and open arms are available
In time of need, we don't have to worry
For GOD is always there to give us His love and mercy.

WHAT'S IN A FRIENDSHIP?

F- orever friends, that's what we are!
R- ain or shine we stick together!
I- n sickness and in health do we part!
E- ndless sharing we are ready to listen!
N- othing in this world can break our vows!
D- o you know that Someone is between us?
S- trengthening our friendship is what He does.
H- ail our Mary, be with us, please continue to
I- ntercede for us and ask His Son JESUS to
P- rotect our friendship and we pray this in
    His name, Amen!

ELIZABETH P. CRISTE . . . WHO IS SHE ?

E- ndurance you have, and you have spiritual energy
L- iving through your faith and you're firm with that
I- nsights you also have and you always share them
Z- eal to serve through taking care of the patients
A- wareness you have, of the Presence of GOD
B- old you are in your conviction, that JESUS is LORD.
E- nthused to learn more about the Almighty
T- enacity you possess especially spiritually
H- umility is one of your greatest assets

P- rudence is another strong quality you have

C- aring you are, as a nurse, daughter, friend and as a sister
R- espectful to everyone, young or old
I- nspiration you are to me
S- elfless and very generous of your time, talent and treasure
T- hank you for being you, my . . .
E- verlasting soul mate.

ANOTHER BEST FRIEND

M- y friend, allow me to say something about you
O- ne of a kind, that's who you are so,
N- ever change a bit, for you are already
A- great friend to me, you are a
L- oving, caring and thoughtful friend, you're an
I- nspiration to your kids and family and with
S- ense of humor, and sensitive to the needs of others
A- nalytical, yes that's another you.

G- reat family you have and you are blessed.

B- eyond everything, you are a trustful person
E- encouraging words, I often hear from you
R- eady to help, a sister to keep and with a
N- urturing instinct as a mother, and you possess that
A- m I blessed or not, having you as my new friend?
B- oldly I can say, "yes I am blessed!"
E- ndearment, my dear friend, I will treasure this forever.

THE 80ᵗʰ BIRTHDAY CELEBRATION of TATAY BERT

Tatay Bert celebrated his 80ᵗʰ birthday this year 2011, in June 26ᵗʰ. I read this poem in front of the relatives and guests. He is like a father to us, (me and Elizabeth.) We honor him and we pray for more blessings in the coming years.

N- ever a dull moment, always with a smile on his face.
O- bligations to his family, he didn't turn his back.
R- esponsiblities he gladly accepts as a family man.
B- rave, he was, facing the youth life maturely.
E- energetic, for his age, A Big 80.
R- espectful to everyone, a real gentleman.
T- ruthful to his wife and a trustworthy employee.
O- pportunity to extend his help, he is keen to that.

C- elebration of life, Happy Birthday with 80 candles.

B- eneath that Big 80, is a young at heart man.
E- njoying life, he shows it, and acknowledges that gift.
R- eminding things for people's benefits is one of his wits.
N- othing can break his principle and he is firm about that.
A- nyone feels comfortable talking to him, for he is very approachable.
B- elieve me, whatever I said about him is his true identity.
E- sther and Elizabeth are his two adopted daughters, giving honor to a wonderful father, the father we have in this foreign country.

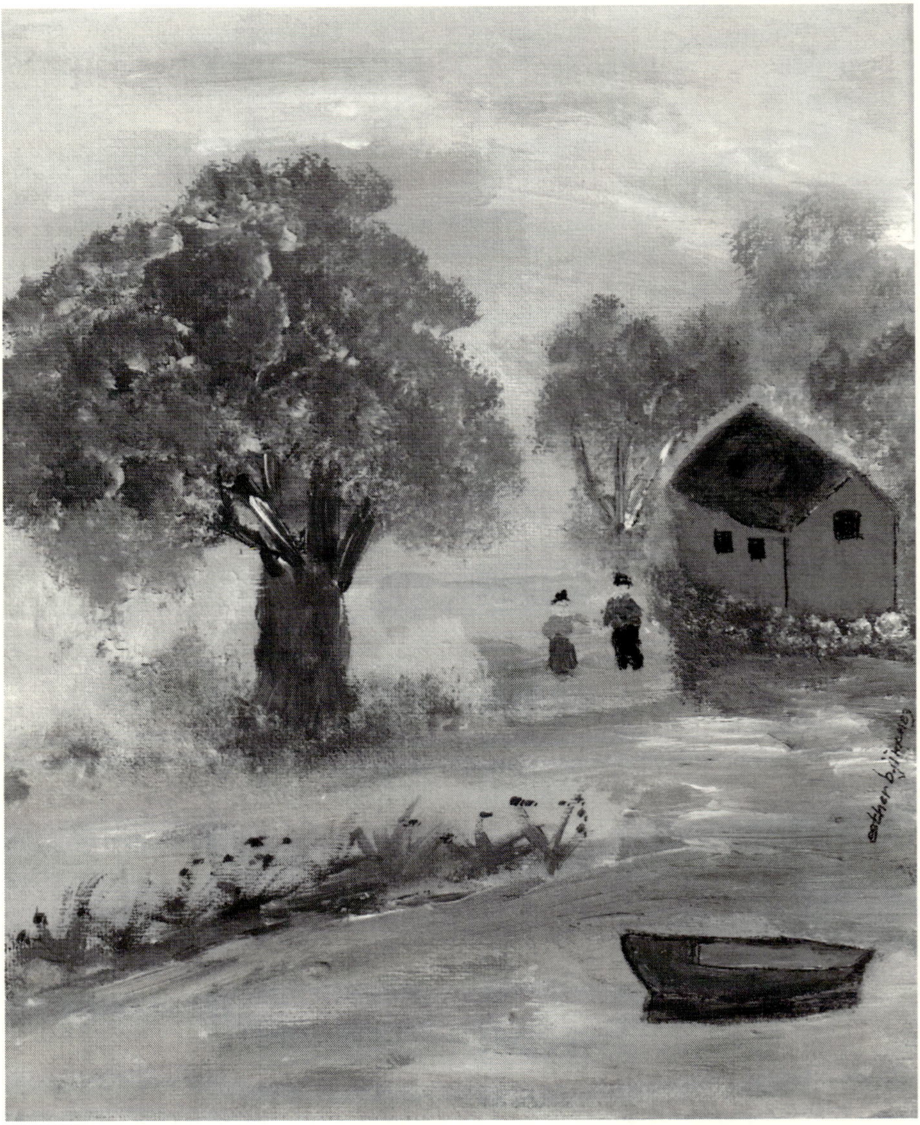

CHAPTER VI

ACRONYMS and HOMONYMS

This whole chapter is about acrostic poems/poetry that described the meaning of the words. Here is what I am talking about . . .

    A- lways use acronyms for memorizing something
    C- ues are important to remember things to accomplish
    R- emembering is the key to memory exercise
    O- bserve things and gather them in your mind
    N- ever give up learning things
    Y- ield to every opportunity, especially education
    M- emorize through lining up the first letters
    S- yllabication is part of learning

When I was in the Nursing school, there were lots of things we have to memorize, from the parts of the human body and its functions, number of bones and more medical terms. We were given a lot of acronyms to facilitate our brain to cope with the lessons. There I was, grew up with my interest in producing, creating words and names, describing them accordingly. This is one way to easily learn things. I threw out some homonyms in this chapter . . . for fun education. It is amazing how the words can give wonderful meanings and it's multiplicities.

Mr. Webster gives us clear definitions of acronym and homonym.

Acronym means a word formed from the initial or letters of each of the successive parts or major parts of a compound term.

Homonym means another name for homophone and homograph; one of two or more words spelled and pronounced alike but different in meaning.

The acronyms in this chapter are also arranged alphabetically.

I encourage you, my dear readers to start utilizing your acrostic wording ability.

You can start with your name and describe yourself and be constructive and positive about yourself.

This is another "WORD GAME," that would help increase our vocabularies.
Enjoy reading the acrostic poems and some homonyms.

DEFINITION OF ABORTION

A- bduction of the innocent fetus from the mother's womb
B- arbaric attitude towards the unborn human being
O- bstruction of human growth
R- idding the most precious human being in this world
T- ransgression, it is against GOD's Law.
I- nfancy Killing
O- ppression of life preservation
N- egative feeling to real meaning of life.

HOW TO PREVENT ABORTION

A- cknowledge the existence of life
B- elieve in GOD and He will guide you until you born the child
O- bey the Ten Commandments, "Thou Shall Not Kill."
R- ooming in the fetus in your womb, is the real comfort zone
T- reat yourself and your child with respect
I- gnore the devil's whispers and devil wishes
O- wing life is saving life, (your mother gives you, your life, therefore you give also life to your child)
N- urture the life that you're carrying and GOD will nurture you.

A- lways guarding us, the angels
N- ever get tired of roaming around
G- uarding is the angels main job
E- choes you heard calling from afar
L- ean on to your angel at your back
S- inging is another angel's way of heralding.

What is the key word to spiritual success? . . . ASK

A- sk
S- eek
K- nock

(Based on Luke 11:9) "And so I say to you: ask and you will receive; Seek and you shall find; knock and the door will be opened to you)

B- elieve in the Holy Bible
I- nspiration you'll have for the
B- ook of the Law is the
L- ife of JESUS CHRIST who'll give us
E- ternal Life and Salvation

B- e still and know that our LORD is GOD
E- ternal Kingdom is at hand
H- eaven is the place that awaits for mankind
O- ur's is the chance to repent
L- et us not waste any moment
D- o invest your time in GOD's business.

* * *

C- all from GOD is scheduled and
H- ope that we'll be called soon
R- enewal is the essence of His call
I- nvitation is fundamental application to
S- elf reflection, an invitation to turn to GOD in
T- ime of chaos and tribulation
I- nspirational words are the words of GOD and the
A- spiration of His call will be our salvation from
N- ow on until our time of call comes along.

C- ommunion with GOD alone
H- allelujah! And songs of praise, GOD's deserves
R- econciliation and forgiveness needs to be done
I- nfant JESUS, incarnated to save us
S- aving us is GOD's utmost love for us.
T- ime to change our lives, for better
M- anger, in a stable, humble JESUS was born
A- ngels sending messages to the shepherds
S- ilence, meditation, contemplation, we have to do, to ponder His Incarnation.

C- aring for kids is a task but must come from the heart
H- ugging them once or more a day is a plus on your part
I- nspirations they are, aren't they?
L- ove, yes of course, is what they need in this world
D- evoting time for tots, is an investment.
R- earing kids is not easy, accepting them is a better deal
E- ntertainers they are, making us happy all year round
N- ever leave your home without saying, "I love you kids."

* * *

D- evote your time in praying
I- nsights, you'll gain as human beings
V- irtues to acquire to be divine
I- nspiration, we have, it's our LORD JESUS
N- ow is the time to work on our divinity
E- ngage your moments to holiness.

D- one and gone from the earth
E- ternal Kingdom awaiting with the angels singing
A- cclaiming our LORD for His love and mercy
T- riumph He grants after tribulation is over
H- eaven, a Holy place where we aspire to go.
May the souls of all departed rest in peace and let the perpetual light shine upon them, especially my parents in whom this book is dedicated.

D- well on good and pleasant memories
E- ducation: like medical treatment and psychotherapy
P- ositive thinking is important
R- ise up from feeling down and keep on living
E- nding life is never a solution
S- adness you will feel, but you can overcome and you will.
S- eek for help, share your feelings and reach out
I- gnore your negative thoughts
O- utlook in life should always be positive
N- ever say there is no treatment for depression, for there is.

* * *

E- verlasting life, there is, beyond, named "heaven."
T- esting our faith to believe, though not seen
E- arthly life we must not dwell
R- emember there is Eternal Kingdom waiting
N- umbers of angels are countless and are
A- waiting for us to join them
L- anding on the clouds level, further up is the heaven.

E- nchanting wings you have
A- ngel's wings you simulate
G- oing and going is what you do
L- ong way to go and long way to search
E- ndless flight you're a might
S- oaring in a changing world is a challenge for you, you're an amazing bird.
(Eagles are mentioned in the Bible)
(Bald eagle is the American symbol of strength and freedom)

E- nchanting personality you have
L- arge family you belong
E- longated tusk you possess
P- ower is your trade mark
H- uge and heavy trunk of yours are amazing
A- frica, India, Ethiopia, Thailand, (places of habitats)
N- ever forget, you're famous for
T- hink Big like elephants is my favorite slogan
S- harp memories you have and I'm fond of you, my animal hero.
(Be a S.T.E.M. Save The Elephant Mammals)
(A pair of elephants was at Noah's ark during the 40 days flood)

* * *

F- ront line, the father is always at . . .
A- ccepts great responsibility to take care of the family
T- eaches his children the right conduct
H- armonious relationship he preserves
E- ducation of the kids, his priority
R- earing partner of a mother.

F- aith is formed by belief and by
A- cquired spiritual knowledge and it
I- nvolves in believing that miracles happened
T- rue believers have great patience and can
H- andle minor and major disappointments.

F- orgiveness you should ask from our LORD
A- ccepting your faults and be sorry for them
I- n your sickness and illness you'll get well, if
T- otally you have strong faith
H- ealing will take place after the ordeal.
(Based on James 5:15) This prayer uttered in faith will reclaim the one who is ill, and the LORD will restore him to health. If he has committed any sins, forgiveness will be his.

True Friendship Is . . .

F- orever mission ready
R- egardless of how busy you are
I- n joy and sorrow, through thick and thin
E- xchange of ideas, learning from each other
N- o one can ruin a true friendship
D- eath do they part, like a vow in marriage
S- ave your friendship, GOD gave this to each other.

F- un hobby it is to fish
I- nteresting people you meet
S- ilence of the water relaxes the mind
H- ands become skill in catching fish
I- nsightful virtues can be obtained through fishing
N- ight or day the fishes are there in the water
G- OD created the fish and other other aquatic species for us mankind to rule over them.

(I love fishing and I can't help but say something about it, but the ironic part is I don't eat fish.) Anyway, fishing in the Bible is better than ordinary fishing as what Mark says, "And JESUS said to them," Follow Me and I will make you become fishers of men . . ." This is a subtle way of evangelization.

PRAYER FOR FORGIVENESS

F- orgive us for our transgressions
O- my LORD,
R- emind us to
G- uard our thoughts and we
I- nvite you in our lives
V- engeance and hatred, take them out from us
E- xchange them with love and humility, Amen!

* * *

G- o to GOD in prayer daily
R- ead GOD's Word everyday
O- bey GOD all the time
W- ords of GOD are powerful
T- rust GOD for everything
H- oly Spirit will aid you in your Spiritual growth.

G- radual feeling that
R- estricts you to have your
I- nsights back . . . but through GOD's
E- nlightenment, you'll be moving
F- orward and no turning back.

Who Is The Holy Spirit?

G- uiding and guarding our thoughts
U- nderstanding, one of His gifts
I- nsight is one of the virtues
D- ependent on the Holy Spirit, we must do
A- dvocate is His other name
N- ever doubt His power
C- onsoler is His another name
E- mpowerment, is the Holy Spirit's engulfing our beings

* * *

H- opes we should have for our daily guidance
O- nly with GOD's grace we can change
L- iving in faith is an answer and
Y- ielding to the Holy Spirit is our hope.
S- ervices we offered, our
P- raises are with You always
I- n GOD's name we thank Thee, for
R- eceiving the gifts of the Holy Spirit
I- nspiring us in our lives daily
T- hank You again LORD for the blessings and graces.

H- anging in there is what they say, and
O- bviously waiting really pays and the
P- romise of GOD is here to be received, so be
E- nlightened with the power of the Holy Spirit
(Based on Romans 15:13)' May GOD, the source of hope, fill you with all joy and peace by means of your faith in Him, so that your hope will continue to grow by the power of the Holy Spirit)

H-and
O-ver your
P-roblems to the
E-xcellent Creator
(Based on Jeremiah 32:37), I am going to gather the people from all the countries where I have scattered them in my anger and fury, and I am going to bring them back to this place and let them live here in safety.)

H- elp, we need and only GOD can provide
E- ver ready, that's how our GOD is
A- bide with the laws and precepts and let's
L- ong for His Presence and it is good enough to heal us forever.
(Based on Psalm 30:2) O, LORD my GOD, I cried out to you and you healed me.)

* * *

I- n Your Presence LORD we feel safe
N- othing is impossible with You
S- ins separate us but Your mercy saves us
I- n the name of JESUS, our Savior who redeems us
G- reat and wonderful You are, our LORD
H- ow we are loved by You, our mighty GOD
T- rusting You we must
S- o LORD give us another chance.

* * *

J- oy in our hearts we always feel, we
E- xalt You our LORD and Your name
S- erving You is our pride and honor
U- ndivided attention we'll give You
S- overeign LORD, You are the Almighty.

J- oy in my heart I always have
E- ndless blessings I receive
S- ufferings and pains, our LORD attained
U- nto His glory we are saved
S- ouls on earth, let's repent and be transformed in the Almighty name, Amen!

J- oseph is Your Father, we
E- nthrone You and Your family
S- orrows Your mother felt during Your passion
U- nderstanding mother You have, thank You for
S- haring her to us, as our Mother too.

J- ESUS is a good Son, as human and as divine
O- bedient to His parents He has proven
S- acrifice His life, He did
E- choes of His pain, her Mother feels
P- arents as they are, Joseph and Mary
H- onoring the Holy Family, we must, as they are part of our family tree.

K-indness, is one great virtue
I-n David's Psalms, kindness mentioned many times
N-ote some random act of kindness and practice them
D- aily, may it be at work, at home or any where
N- ever miss to say "thank you", everyday
E- ngage in any program for promoting kindness
S-mile all the time, that's kindness
S- end someone a card or a friendly note if you can or for just keeping in touch.

K- ind, great, good, awesome GOD, I praise You my LORD
I- honor You with profound reverence
N- ight and day, I will offer my prayers
G- rant me LORD, the graces I need, You are the King of Kings

                *   *   *

L- ove yourself and love others is the meaning of life
I- nspiration is the meaning of life
F- ear of death is the meaning of life, but life after death is an
E- ndless meaning of life.

L- iving in the Holy Spirit
I- n the name of JESUS CHRIST
F- ather thank you for
E- verything you've done in my life.
(Based on Deuteronomy 30:19) I call heaven and earth today
to witness against you: I have set before you life and death,
the blessing and the curse. Choose life, then that you and
your descendants may live, . . .

L- ove is everlasting and the elements are
O- bedience and sharing one another and giving
V- alue, honor and respect to each other
E- mbrace, hug and warm touch are gestures of love.

L- ORD, our GOD, You're our Savior
O- ur praises and thanksgiving are forever
V- otive candles we must offer
E- ternal love we aspire

OUR LORD . . .

L- ights our ways and all the
A- ngles of our lives and we'll
M- ove towards Your direction for
P- rotection from any harm.
*(Based on 2 Samuel 22:29) You are my lamp, O, LORD
the LORD turns my darkness into light.*

L- et me learn your ways
O- h LORD
R- emember me all the time
D- ear LORD, and I'll
S- ing praises all my life
P- ardon me for my wrong doings
R- epent, I need to do
A- ccept me LORD as your servant
Y- ielding for your laws, I'll do and
E- nhance my faith, O, LORD, I will
R- ecite the LORD's Prayer from my heart not from my mouth,
  I must do.

* * *

M- eet the challenges in life
I- n the most troubled times
R- ecollection of the past of how we survived
A- wareness we must have, of GOD's mystery
C- HRIST is the only answer for everything
L- ong before you know
E- ndless miracles are happening within
S- aving us is one great mystery and more miracles to come, just
  wait and see.

M- inding the business and affairs of her children, the very role of a mother
O- ffers the best service she can, to suffice each child's needs
T- riumph and success, she wishes for all her kids
H- eartaches she often feels, but hidden, for that is what a typical mother is
E- motions as love and care she gives through out her life
R- emembering and honoring her are the essential gifts we can offer in return.

M- y LORD, I pray Thee that I may
E- mbrace Your law and follow them
R- ighteousness will bring me to be
C- loser to You and and
Y- our mercy will be poured upon me.
(Based on James 2:13) For GOD will not show mercy when He judges the person who has not been merciful, but mercy triumphs over the judgment.

M- an of GOD, leader of the Hebrews
O- bedience is what he strongly possessed, he
S- aved the Hebrews from the hands of the Egyptian slavery
E- ndless power and help, GOD gave him to
S- how Pharaoh (the Egyptian leader), the power of GOD

* * *

N- ightingale maiden, the humble servant of humanities
U- niversally celebrated, the Nurses Week, it is
R- ecognition, yes, needed as reward for their achievements
S- olemnly pledged to take care of the clients of any creed
E- nergy and tenacity, two physical qualities nurses' possess
S- alute, we do, to honor you all, Nurses on this special week.

N- ever a dull moment
U- nder stress at times
R- otating shift she works
S- alary wages, pretty good
E- ngage in different nursing fields
S- haring their lives to serve.

* * *

O- pportunity to serve, is rewarding
B- ecause you're doing it for GOD, in return for His
E- ndless blessings
D- aily prayer time should be set
I- n our lives and let us
E- ncourage our brothers and sisters to do the same.
N- othing is impossible for whatever we do, if we just
C- oncentrate on GOD's possibilities and He'll
E- nhance our faith and belief.

If you need help, call 1-800 P R A Y E R S (listed only in heaven)

P- raise GOD
R-ejoice for GOD
A- scribe to GOD
Y- ield to GOD
E- xalt GOD
R- epent for GOD
S- erve GOD
(Based on Mark 11:24) I give you my word, if you are ready to believe that you will receive whatever you ask for in prayer, it shall be done for you.

P- rayers are powerful
R- egardless of whether you're at home or anywhere
A- cknowledge the existence of GOD and
Y- ou'll feel His Presence
E- ngage yourself in the habit of praying and you'll feel the
R- ichness of your life and the
S- pirituality within you.
(Based on the book entitled "Prayers From The Prison.")

P- ray at all times
R- ejoice and be glad everyday
A- lleluia ! To the King of Kings!
I- ndestructible Kingdom our LORD's
S- on Has and
E- verybody should honor and praise Him.

P- romise of peace will be with us, so just
E- ntrust everything to GOD for He always sends
A- ngels to guard us and guide our ways, so let's
C- alm down and rest assured that
E- ndless help and forever peace will be poured upon us.
(Based on John 14:27) Peace I leave you with; my peace give you as the world gives. Do not let your hearts be troubled and do not be afraid.

P- ure heart our LORD has
E- ndless love He gives us
R- edeeming us is one of His plans
F- orgiving us more than seventy times
E- mbracing us in times of loneliness
C- alling us when our time comes
T- ruly our LORD is Perfect, flawless and accurate, thank You LORD for creating us.
(Based on 2 Samuel 22:31) "As for GOD, his way is perfect; the Word of the LORD is flawless. He is a shield for all who take refuge in him.

P- ositive
A- ttitude and acceptance of the loss
L- etting go of the past
S- tart a new life.
After you grieved be PALS to yourselves.

* * *

Q- ueen of angels, queen of martyrs is our Blessed Mother
U- nity of heart, we must have for the queen
E- ndless intercessor, our Mother is
E- nlightening us, she does for the coming of His Son JESUS
N- ativity, is a beautiful scene of the Holy Family.

R- adiant colors that lighten our lives
A- rk shape you have, that covers the earth
I- nspiration you are, rainbow reflection
N- owhere to find your beginning and your end but you have
B- right colors, with variations and each with symbols
O- bviously you're one of GOD's creations
W- indows should be open when the rainbow appears, to welcome one of GOD's wonders.

* * *

The SAME MAN forever

S- aving us
A- ll the time
M- an of Honor, our GOD Is!
E- xtending His Hands all over the world.
(Based on Hebrews 13:8) "JESUS is the same yesterday, today and forever.

WHO IS JESUS?

S- infulness, the reason He redeems us
A- cknowledges our frailties
V- ery forgiving
I- am one of the sinners that He saves
O- ffers Himself, His everything
R- edeemer, Refuge, the Resurrected One.

S- triving for your goals
U- ntil you reach them
C- aring not only for your job but for the people
C- ompassion a great virtue to hold on
E- xtend extra miles, that's a plus
S- uccess can be attained, with GOD's grace, including your
S- kills and other assets.

S- acrifice,
U- nderstanding,
C- oncern,
C- are,
E- nlightenment,
S- suddenly,
S- prouted.
These are the KEYS to successful relationship.

* * *

T- errific Day to celebrate
H- appy moments to ponder
A- bundance to be thankful for
N- ever ending blessings we receive
K- ind hearted people are there, everywhere
S- ing and Praise for today is a special day
G- OD, who else is the Only Source of health and strength
I- mportant day to remember every year
V- oices, GOD hears and He listens very well
I- nvite GOD and feel His Presence
N- ote down the graces and acknowledge them
G- reat Day, isn't it? May I greet you a Happy Thanksgiving Day.
D-ear GOD, thank You for Your
A- bundance and protection
Y- ou are an awesome and great GOD. We love You and we bless You, too.

T- ruth is
R- evealed and
U- nfolded by the
S- pirit of
T- he LORD, the
S- overeign One.

T- emple is the place to worship and
E- ngage in sharing the
M- oments of Truth by
P- raying and praising
L- onging for GOD's call and
E- mbracing His will.
*(Based on Mark 11:17) Then he began to teach them:
"Does not Scripture have it, My house shall be called
a house of prayer for all peoples'-? but you have turned
it into a den of thieves.*

* * *

U- nspoken words, divine actions, effective evangelization
N- ote down good points, from a righteous person
I- nspiration, insight derive from motivational people
T- eachings, testimonies are the best teachers
Y- earning to be united with the Sovereign One and to give divine lessons.

* * *

VETERAN'S ACRONYM

A- mazing country United States is!
M- any immigrants are being welcomed every year
E- agle is one of the symbols of America that signifies strength and freedom
R- adiant stars in the American flag boldly represents 52 States
I- integrity and dignity, the virtues that American soldiers possess.
C- ountry and land of liberty, that's America!
A-m I proud to be an American? You bet, I am!

V- ictorious, vibrant, these American soldiers are
E- nergetic and enthusiastic to fight
T- riumph is their goal in the armed force
E- ndangering their lives and always at
R- isk every moment of their lives
A- iming to win in every battle
N- ever to surrender until peace is attained.
S- alute to all American soldiers.

V- ows to defend the beloved country
E- ndless prayers we should offer
T- ime will come the war will end
E- verywhere, the veterans are honored on this special day, Veterans Day!
R- endering service is a noble virtue
A- wareness of the Veteran's Day is essential
N- ever should we forget how the veterans fought
S- ervice for the country is a heroic deed.
D- eceased or alive, the veterans must be recognized in our hearts
A- rmy, Navy, Marine, Coast Guards, Airforce and every military group must be remembered on this special day.
Y- ou and I should know the value of men and women in uniform.

V- ictory over the vileness and viciousness of evil force, we must celebrate
O- verwhelming feeling for the triumphs achieved
W- oe! To the wicked for they failed to acknowledge the vow of GOD in the Ark of the Covenant.

* * *

W- e need our guardian angels to watch us
I- n times of distress
N- ever allow anybody to break our
G- uardian Angel's wings
S- o LORD thank You for our angels who watch us every step of the way.

* * *

MY X's PRAYER

LORD, I worship and honor You. I eXalt Your name.
I am just an ordinary person LORD, but I want to do eXtraordinary thing, to eXtend another mile, in my service to You.
I thank You for the gifts that You have given me.
Help me to X-out (cross-out) the things I don't need in life, all the eXcess baggages.
Guide me every step of the way and help me in eXamining my conscience. LORD, I offer to You my frailties and weaknesses. Grant me LORD the spiritual strength for my spiritual growth and spiritual pathway,
In JESUS name, Your EXCELLENCY, I pray, Amen!

Y-et to come, yet not prepared
O-ur LORD JESUS, will come any moment
K- ing of Kings, our GOD is
E-ndless praising we need to do for the endless blessings.

* * *

Z- echariah, a Hebrew prophet, father of John the Baptist
E- lizabeth his wife, cousin of Virgin Mary
A- ngels appeared in them in different occasions
L- ORD, thank You for the prominent people, the Anointed ones.

THE GIFT OF MORTIFICATION

M- any a sin of Your servants on earth
O- bedience is a start, O poor souls need to repent
R- oad to salvation, the way to transformation
T- ransformation, the pathway to holiness
I- nfinite love of JESUS will be received
F- aith and trust in GOD must be implanted in our hearts
I- mage of GOD is our true identity
C- HRIST JESUS, is the Sovereign One, who heals our souls through eternity
A- doration in front of the Blessed Sacrament, as to offering our all
T- rials and tribulations we must also be thankful
I- nner healing is the gift that will come back to us countless folds
O- ffering back to GOD our afflictions and ailments
N- othing is impossible to attain, including the Holy Spirit's gift of mortification.

NOW IS THE TIME TO PLAY WITH THE WORDS OF HOMONYMS . . . Let's start with . . .

BILL

His name is **Bill** a neighbor of Jill, who is writing a check to pay his **bill.** He is a good citizen, exercising his rights, including the **Bill of Rights.** Do you have another word for **bill?**
"Yes I do," the bird answered, how about my **bill?**

THE TRUNK

There is a chest **trunk** found in an island, dropped beneath the tree **trunk** by a huge elephant, carried with his **trunk.** Then a guy in a swimming **trunk** saw the chest **trunk** and bending his body and **trunk,** he put the chest **trunk** in the **trunk** of his car.
The chest **trunk** in question has a **trunk** load of wisdom to use in this world.

A BEAR

A huge **bear** is pregnant and she is about to **bear** the infant she is carrying. She **bears** the pain and very patiently waiting, until the baby comes out and it'll be a relief on her part.
A family of **bears** visit and **bear** gifts for the mother **bear. Bears** are also with human hearts and compassion. Our GOD created them as well and we should treat them like humans.
To create is to **bear** fruits for human and animal as well.

THE BAR

A lawyer who just passed the **bar** exam visited his client in the prison's **bar.** The case happened in the club **bar** where his client works.
His client had hurt a co-worker as self-defense, using a crow **bar** found near the sink where the **bar** of soap was. Luckily the lawyer won the case. What a relief on the client's side.
"I think I need to have a candy **bar,** for I lost a good amount of sugar during the court hearing," the lawyer uttered. At least there are two things that the lawyer did for his client. One is, no more **bar** action, meaning no destruction of the client's reputation, and second, he won't be wearing a **bar**-like (stripes of black and white uniform) in the prison.
Did I forget another **bar** word?
There are two **bars** not significant to the lawyer's case. (the swiping of the **bar** code and the **bar** of gold.)
At least, I came up with fourteen **bars**, and this is the shortest story ever told, in the **bar** world.

THE TIP

A young man was walking near the **tip** disposal, a (place to dump rubbish). He was rushing to go to work as a waiter, few miles from his house. He met his co-worker outside and he gave him **tip** to hurry-up, because the manager is **tipped** off for he is late again. So he went inside and proceeded to his locker **tiptoeing,** hanged his hat at the **tip** of the wooden pole.
The manager spotted him and told him to leave and he was suspended for few days. That night he lost good amount of **tips** from the customers.
Here is my **tip** for the waiter, "Be not late for you'll lose more **tips.**"

THE WELL

Well, let me see if I could come up with more **wells** in this anecdote. Wish me **well**, because I have to form the word **well** accordingly and to make sure it is **well** fit to my story.

I don't know if I need to wish from a **well** spring or a **well** along the damp road or maybe a real wishing **well** in the fantasy island. I think I need to pump **well** my brain muscles to come up with more **wells.**

Mr. Webster gives a lot of meaning of the word **well**, but I just want few words, coming from my point of view. I mean **wel**l don't get me wrong. Will somebody say, "**Well** said and done and a job **well** done." Now, I have mentioned a lot of **wells** and I think I need to rest for a while and again, wish me **well** please. Thank you my dear readers for listening **well.**

DRIVE

A five letter word that I need to dissect in order for me to create a short essay. Most of us when we hear the word, **drive** we think of a vehicle, a truck or a car in motion. I have this **drive** to elaborate more of this **drive** business, as in a **drive**r teaching a person how to **drive.** Sometimes when a **drive**r teaches people how to **drive** professionally, he can't help but to be stressed, it **drive**s him nuts, especially for the stubborn ones. Students should have the **drive** to learn fast and be safe. If the student has the right attitude in **drivi**ng he will have good **drive** miles.

By the way the student he is teaching now doesn't need to pay him because he will teach his teacher how to use the computer **drive.** So this is an exchange **drive** (deal), **drive** a bargain.

My reminder for the teacher **drive**r and the student **drive**r, "**Drive** carefully and don't drink and **drive.**" Have a successful **drivi**ng lesson. Let's **drive** out the negative force when holding the wheel.

To **drive** or not to **drive**, that is my drive essay.

THE BIT

This is a story of a horse who is about to join the race. The jockey checked his mouth to see the bridle, if its **bit** (a steel part of the bridle inserted in horse's mouth), is in place. He takes care of his horse especially his food and that's why he feeds him **bit** by **bit** to protect his teeth with the inserted **bit**, for further damage.
He is a little **bit** worried, because lately his horse was not eating well and found out that he accidentally **bit** a scrap metal. The vet advised the jockey to let the horse rest a **bit** until he regains his strength. More tidbits next time my dear readers.

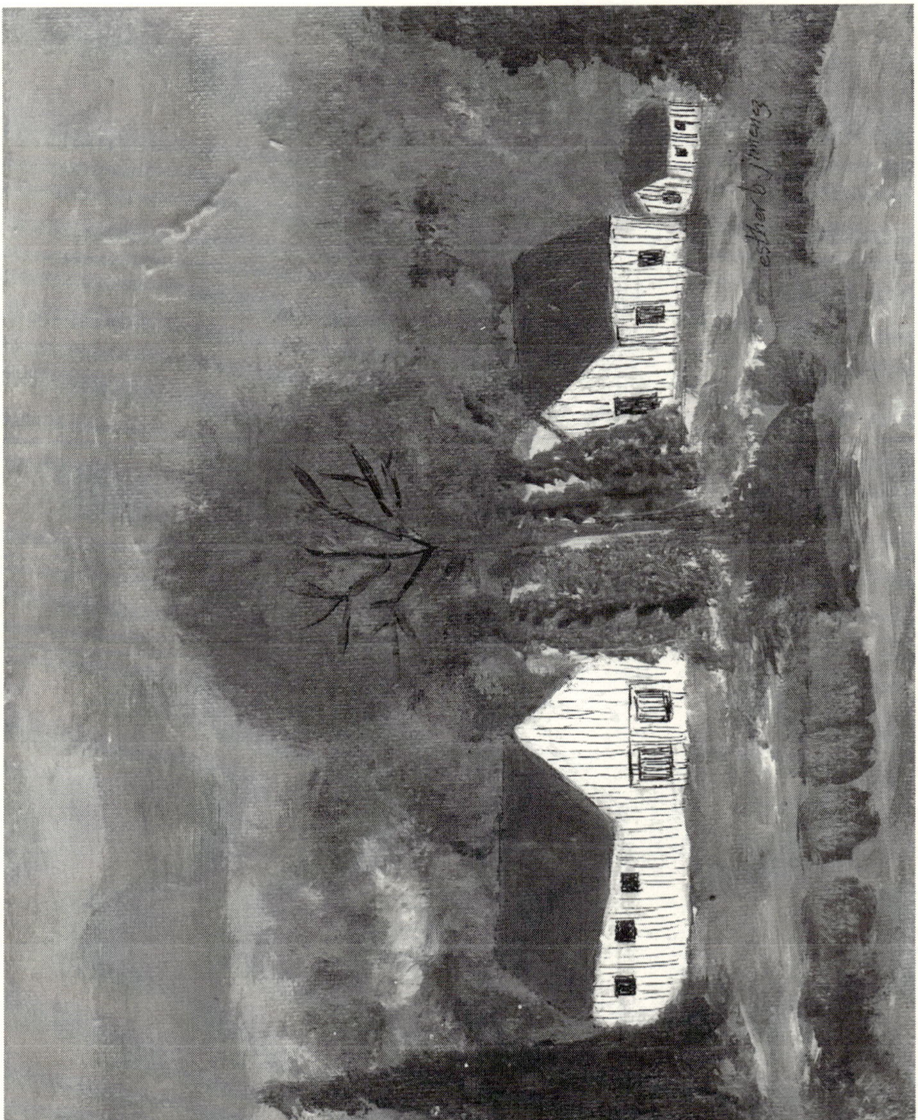
esther b. Jimenez

CHAPTER VII

THE ABC'S

The A B C chapter is about guiding us through the proper sequence of information given. We learn the basic language and its formation from the A B C, as in 1 2 3 for the numbers. Everyone and everything "start from the very beginning." sounds familiar? Yes, it's from the musical movie, "The Sound Of Music". A poem/poetry that formatted from A B C is an easy way to relate with our interest in reading. It's also easy to memorize with the A B C as the guide. The A B C of learning is the X Y Z of fulfilling, learning the simple and basic rules in life.

BEATITUDES . . .

(THE A B C OF THE "BE ATTITUDE")

Be- Accommodating and be approachable, for you'll be respected.
Be- Bold in your conviction, for you'll be given more wisdom.
Be- Compassionate and Caring, for things will be smoothly handled.
Be- Delightful with all your blessings, and more blessings will come.
Be- Enthusiastic in learning GOD's Word, for wisdom is at hand.
Be- Forgiving, for GOD's love and mercy will be poured upon you.
Be- Grateful all the time, for GOD's graces will be returned, hundred folds.
Be- Humble in deeds and words, for peace will be in your heart forever.
Be- Insightful with the Word of the LORD, for proper guidance will be yours.
Be- Joyful in GOD's glory, for joy will be attained in the Eternal Kingdom.
Be- Kind to everyone, for it'll produce pleasant relationship.
Be- Loving all the time, most of all to GOD, for it is the greatest love of all.
Be- Merciful for GOD is merciful, meek and humble.
Be- Nice, simple as that, for life is too short and it deserves gentle treatment.
Be- Open and optimistic in handling your problems, for GOD is there to help.
Be- Prayerful, the best of all "Be Attitude," for prayer is a powerful tool.
Be- Quiet in times of your solitude and know that GOD is there.
Be- Repentant of your soul searching, for you'll attain a valid answer.
Be- Sacred and Holy, for in Holiness there is peace.
Be- Truthful and honest, for the Truth will set you free.
Be- Unearthly and less vain, for it will aid you to a better life style.
Be- Vigilant, for you'll never know when the silent thief will come.
Be- Willing to serve, for servanthood is a step to sainthood.
Be- X-tra somebody, for extending miles is a plus for your transformation.
Be- Yourself, be not someone else, for GOD created you in His Image.
Be- Zealous in your faith in all aspects, for it will lead you to Holiness.

If you put this A B C of BE Attitude in your heart and mind, you'll have a fruitful, blessed, and peaceful life.

THE A B C OF MOTHERHOOD

A- mother is a model of all cares
B- ecause of the time she shares.
C- aring for the husband and the kids as well
D- ay to day, she never misses to
E- ncourage her kids to do their best.
F- airness among the kids, she tries to be
G- enuine heart she has, kids should know that
H- onoring a mother from time to time just for being her.
I- ndeed she'll be thrilled and will treasure it forever.
J- oy and happiness, she always feels though
K- ids personalities and age differ
L- ove and care, her favorite two words
M- other that she is, can never be compared
N- o dull moments the kids are . . . to her
O- verwhelming situation, she is always in
P- ride she has, when talking about her kids
Q- ueries here and there, all she hears
R- ole of a mother is a sacrifice, but commendable
S- afety measures, she practices them all
T- rue enough, the mother is the first teacher
U- nderstanding her pupils at home really matters
V- ersatility, one of her great assets
W-oman as she is, never to be ignored
X- cellent job, performs by this motherhood role
"Y-es mommy", she often hears and loves it, so
Z- oom her little tasks, and surface them, if we must,
"Mother Of The Year" all these mothers deserved.

THE A B C OF PERSONAL GROWTH

A- cquire knowledge from anyone and everywhere
B- reak the old habits
C- onvince yourself that you can do it
D- ivide your activities properly
E- ngage on positive thoughts
F- ear not . . . all the challenges in life
G- rab all the best opportunities you can have
H- andle everything cautiously
I- nsight . . . you should have in every transaction
J- oin the positive group of people
K- ind heart and gentleness you should possess, you got it made
L- ove . . . you should have for everything you do
M- ind our own business is a good practice
N- etwork with positive thinkers
O- pportunity is everywhere, just be open
P- ositive attitude will give positive results
Q- uantify and qualify your prospects, career, friend or any aspect
R- emember the Golden Rule all the time
S- piritual strength is needed in every way and in everything
T- hink positive as they always say, mind you it works, try it anyway
U- niqueness you have, you should claim it and be proud of it
V- iew all the facts before you surrender to commitment
W- ean yourself from unpleasant relationship
X- "x" as the sign says, eliminate, cross-out negative thoughts
Y- ield to any approaching risk in your life
Z- one all your areas of strength and use them wisely.

THE A B C OF THE HOLY SPIRIT

A- dvocate is Your another name and we are
B- lessed to have You in our lives
C- ountless gifts that we received, and we should
D- ivinely use them and we should
E- njoy the gifts of a lifetime.
F- ear of GOD is one of Your gifts, and You
G- uide us to attain this, O,
H- oly Spirit You are awesome and
I- nfinite, we honor You with profound reverence
J- oy in our hearts we feel knowing You are there
K- nowledge of You is a mystery
L- ife in the Spirit is the best way to live
M- any trials and tribulations await, but
N- othing can set us apart, O Holy Spirit
O- bstacles may surround us, but the
P- eace that You grant, is the weapon we have
Q- uest to know You more is our deepest desire
R- everence of Your Presence is our utmost response
S- pirit of love and Spirit of mercy, we
T- rust in GOD, the LORD JESUS, the Holy Spirit
U- nited with us O Holy Trinity and also with the
V- irgin Mary, the Blessed Immaculate One
W- ords so powerful, gifts so wonderful, how
X- cellent is GOD's plan with Your prompts
Y- es, LORD JESUS, thank You for giving us Your Advocate, who
Z- ooms our humanity to divinity.

THE ALPHABET CHRISTIAN WISDOM

A- ll things are possible to GOD
B- ible is the source of wisdom
C- hristian or non- Christian are united in heart
D- aily prayers are essential
E- ndless blessings, we are given
F- ather on earth is Our Father in Heaven
G- OD the LORD, conquers all
H- allelujah! Praise the LORD
I- nfinite power, our Almighty possesses
J- ESUS, the Son of GOD, is our Redeemer
K- ingdom of Heaven, the place we should aim
L- ove one another and love GOD above all
M- ary, the Blessed Virgin Mother is our model of perfection
N- ever doubt the power of GOD at all
O- mnipotent, omniscient, omnipresent, omnificent, that's how powerful our GOD is
P- rayers! Prayers! Are powerful weapons
Q- uietness is needed for productive meditation
R- ejoice and glorify the LORD
S- ing aloud and magnify the LORD's name
T- ruth will set you free
U- nion with GOD is what we need
V- ictory over abomination is a celebration
W- ord of GOD must be in our hearts.
X- cellent job GOD did, creating us in His Image
Y- ield to GOD's plan and follow His pathway
Z- ealous and great GOD we have, isn't He wonderful?

THE A B C OF CATHOLIC CHRISTIAN

A- ngels we all have and always watching us
B- rothers and sisters united in CHRIST
C- hristians are believers of CHRIST JESUS
D- aughters of GOD, we women on earth
E- ucharistic Adoration, the best meditation
F- ather, our LORD GOD, the Father of all
G- reat, good and generous that's Who our GOD is
H- eaven and earth are filled with GOD's glory
I- con, not idolatry, but respect for tradition and history
J- ESUS, Mary and Joseph, the model family
K- ing of Kings, our LORD the name above all names
L- amb of GOD takes away the sins of the world
M- erciful and forgiving is the Sovereign One
N- uns and priests are anointed people with special vows
O- bedience of the laws, precepts and decrees are important for transformation
P- ardon of sins and absolution by priest is done at Sacrament of reconciliation
Q- uest for the truth, seek for the truth and the Truth is JESUS
R- osary recited daily from five to twenty decades will please our Mother Mary
S- acraments seven of them, must be received by the faithful ones
T- rust we should have, on the teachings of Catholics Cathecism
U- niversal, this is the meaning of Catholicism
V- ictory is with us, conquering all evil whispers
W- e can overcome everything through GOD's grace
X- exalt His name, we must honor Him with profound reverence
Y- earning for a deeper relationship with JESUS a Christian goal
Z- igzag road is not the road to salvation. There's only one road. It's a straight pathway . . . GOD's Way!

ACCLAMATION! (THE A B C OF WORSHIP)

We worship You, O LORD, the	ALMIGHTY!
We owe You our lives, You are our	BENEFACTOR!
In Your Image we are created great	CREATOR!
You redeemed us,	DIVINE SAVIOR!
We bow down to You,	ETERNAL FATHER!
Our delight is in You, our	FORTRESS!
In the dark, You are our	GUIDING LIGHT!
You saved us our	HOLY REDEEMER!
You are always there, the	INFINITE!
You are our sorrow and	JOY!
In our hearts, You're the	KING OF KINGS!
We acknowledge You as the	LAMB OF GOD!
In Zion, You' re the	MIGHTY KING!
You are the Name above all	NAMES!
You are everywhere	OMNIPRESENT!
You always heal us, You're our	PHYSICIAN!
You are loved by our Mother, the	QUEEN!
You are the Risen LORD, the	RESURRECTION!
You are our Shepherd, our great	SAVIOR!
You taught us to be obedient, our	TEACHER!
You are the King of the	UNIVERSE!
You are the Truth, the Way and the	VINE!
You're an awesome GOD, our	WAKE-UP CALLER!
You are perfect and	X- CELLENT!
You are the LORD GOD, our	YAHWEH!
You are the most powerful and the most	ZEALOUS ONE!

LORD, AS LONG AS I LIVE, I WILL PRAISE YOU FOREVER!

THE A B C FOR HOSPICE VOLUNTEERS

A- cknowledge the client's needs
B- ring a Bible, books or any materials to read
C- aring with compassion we must render
D- on't hesitate to extend your miles further
E- ncourage the client for verbalization
F- or expressing one's self and mental stimulation
G- races you'll attain for just taking care of the client
H- old the client's hands, let them feel your warmth
I- ndeed, as volunteers, we are appreciated
J- oy, they feel and they are comforted
K- ind words, the client needed to hear
L- ove from their kins, they wanted them near
M- eeting the families, is essential, for an extension of our care
N- eed to inform the families, of the client's requests
O- ffering the service with sufficient hospice knowledge
P- rogress of the client, the volunteers must know
Q- uestions we might ask, to know more about the clients
R- equests and lists of wishes, the clients might express
S- afety measures, the volunteers must observe
T- alking and communicating is essential for better care
U- nderstanding each other's situations is important
V- olunteers must view the fact about death and dying,
W- ith the coordinators and other hospice team
X- er-cise ethics and professionalism in the hospice ministry,
Y- ou, me, the client, the family and must have teamwork
Z- oning the areas of individuality is, valuable for volunteers.

THE A B C FOR THE NEW YEAR

A- lways believe in the Almighty, Who will be your guide for all the years
B- e not afraid of GOD, for He keeps His promises
C- HRIST—centered and Christian values are the keys to transformation
D- elightful it is, to serve GOD all the time, even in every little ways
E- nrichment of the soul is the core of life relationship
F- ellowship with one another is a fellowship with our LORD
G- ifts of the Holy Spirit are within us, we just have to unwrap them
H- oliness is for everyone, be holy, because GOD is Holy
I- mitate JESUS' divinity, have a holy intimacy with Him
J- ESUS is the reason for the season, and He is the center of our hearts.
K- eep in your heart the good deeds you did the past year, and utilize them again for the coming year
L- ove is always needed for good, harmonious relationship
M- ake amends for your wrong doings and make a pathway to forgiveness
N- ever give up hope. Hope is a virtue that keep us alive
O- vercome the obstacles in life by offering everything to our Almighty
P- rayers are powerful weapons to use to combat the abominations here on earth
Q- uestions in life are essential. They lead us to truthfulness and the facts of life
R- esolutions are made for transformation. They are guidelines for reformation
S- eek GOD's help in every difficulties that cross your way
T- ell the truth, for the truth will set you free
U- nderstanding oneself and understanding others lead to knowing more of our Sovereign One
V- ictory is with us when we have GOD in our lives, who can be against us?
W- ords are powerful when spoken from the heart
X- cellent GOD we have, we should remember that, and no one can beat His power
Y- early we must evaluate our performances and check if they are in accordance with GOD's will.
Z- ealous for GOD is one of the best virtues to cultivate in life.

THE A B C OF . . . HOW TO PRAY

Pray with **Adoration** . . .   I worship and honor You LORD with profound reverence and I magnify Your name.

Pray with **Benevolence** . . .   I bow down to You with my knees on the ground, to show You my respect and reverence

Pray with **Contrition** . . .   LORD, I ask for Your love and mercy, and for Your constant forgiveness for all my sins and wrong doings and the things I failed to do as a true Christian.

Pray with **Divinity** . . .   LORD, I pray for holiness in my life. I offer to You my humanness, that I may be divine in my ways.

Pray with **Exaltation** . . .   I exalt Your name, glorify You through my songs and my playing guitar, tuning the Christian worship songs.

Pray with **Faith** . . .   I surrender everything to You my LORD without any doubt, and that You may hear and listen. I know from my heart that You'll guide me always.

Pray with **Gratitude** . . .   I thank You for everything my LORD, for the gifts of the Holy Spirit and the gift of life.

Pray with **Humility** . . .	LORD, I know that I can't do anything without You. I am a sinner and I need Your graces and be more repentant.
Pray with **Intercession** . . .	I pray for all the souls in Purgatory, for the people who are asking to pray for them and for those who have no one to pray for them.
Pray with **Joy** . . .	LORD, there is delight in my heart knowing You are there to guide me all the time.
Pray with **Kindness** . . .	LORD, grant me the gift of Random Act Of Kindness, that I may be able to extend help to others and even to strangers.
Pray with **Love** . . .	LORD, love is a powerful tool to any relationship. I am blessed with the love of my family and friends. Thank You my LORD for Your unconditional love and the love of Your Son, JESUS.
Pray with **Meditation** . . .	I always crave for my conversation with You LORD. I always feel Your utmost Presence when I meditate. Meditating Your Word is powerful. LORD grant me moments of solitude with You.

Pray with **Never-Ending prayers** ...	LORD, few times the phrase unceasing prayers are mentioned in the Bible. Yes it is essential to pray unceasingly because it is our way of life.
Pray with **Obedience** ...	LORD I pray to be more obedient with my undertakings, like Your Holy Ten Commandments. May You grant me the gift of fasting on Lent seasons, and help me in my thoughts of justification. I honor our Blessed Mother Mary for her utmost obedience.
Pray with **Praise** ...	LORD, to praise You is to honor You, to worship You with our utmost reverence. We profoundly acclaim Your kindness, greatness and goodness. I praise You for everything and everyday with my humble gratitude.
Pray with **Quest** ...	LORD, my Holy Quest is to know You more and to have a holy intimate relationship with You. I pray LORD to be more holy and be more repentant and I need Your grace to fulfill that.
Pray with **Reverence** ...	LORD, I thank You for the gift of prayer. A prayer without reverence is not effective as with reverence. I pray for the gifts of the Holy Spirit.

Pray with **Supplication** . . .	LORD, thank You for answering our prayers. Again, the Holy Spirit says, "Ask and you shall receive." I earnestly and humbly ask for Your love and and mercy. Let us feel Your Presence wherever we are and whatever we do.
Pray with **Thanksgiving** . . .	LORD, together with our unceasing prayers are our unceasing gratitude for everything. I thank You for the gift of life, the gift of family, friends, and community. Most of all I thank You for the gifts of the Holy Spirit.
Pray with **Understanding** . . .	LORD, You are the most understanding of all in this world that You created. I pray for the gift of understanding, that I may think of others first, before myself and to love them unconditionally.
Pray with **Virtues** . . .	LORD, I know praying with virtues needs Your grace. I pray that You may grant me virtues to use in dealing with my daily endeavors. Help us cultivate virtues for a better relationship with one another.
Pray with **Willingness** . . .	LORD, You have granted us the freedom to pray, but we have to have willingness of heart to pour out our concerns. I thank You for allowing me to surrender my being, and the willingness of letting You know I give in, to Your power over us.

Pray with **X-citement** . . .   LORD, there is delight and joy in my heart whenever I am at the chapel or church especially in front of the Blessed Sacrament. I know that excitement is not jumping for joy, but heart pounding for Your Presence. I thank You my LORD for the reasons to be joyful, Your utmost Presence.

Pray with **Yearning** . . .   LORD, I am hungry for Your Word. I always look forward to have a conversation with You. I yearn for Your love, and thank You for Your Presence.

Pray with **Zeal** . . .   LORD JESUS, I pray that You will grant me more spiritual tenacity, so I can be of service to You. I love to serve You, the way You wanted to be served. Allow me to serve You with zealousness, with my fervent prayers.

Here's another A B C that I would like to share. Actually, I have already submitted the manuscript when I found this poem in my old briefcase. It was a poem with ABC format written by my nephew, Francis. He dedicated this poem to me and I can't help but to share it with you, my dear readers. I must say that I am flattered by his kind thoughts about me. He wrote this poem with sincerity of heart and profound love. He handed this poem last year, (2010.) Thank you my nephew and I'm proud of you. I wrote a poem about him when he was 8 years old and it is included in this book, Francis has written at least fifty poems himself, soon to be published, too.

THE ALPHABET OF ESTHER

A- rtist, adviser . . . in every stroke of her brush, shows the color of her sides, as deep as her advices, as strong as the ocean tides.
B- odyguard . . . she's everyone's protector, ready to battle war, she's guardian by your side, watching over from afar.
C- hef, collector . . . finder of new recipes, a cook for satisfaction, human vault of beauty of crafts, of grand collection.
D- ecision Maker . . . a firm disposition she has, pursuing a single road, with certainty and valor, a true marked of an endowed.
E- valuator . . . appreciative of good things, a critic with good judgment, aura of her womanhood.
F- riend, fisher . . . her spirit of attraction, magnet of companionship, hooking both comrades and fish, she reels the rod of friendship.
G- ame player . . . she's game all time and a sporty, a winner, a champion she's witty.
H- istorian . . . her memory of the past, a lesson for the future, time traveler might she be, a teacher of wise lecture.
I- rresistible lady . . . as charming as she is now, as attractive as she'll be, her words of endearment, is something one cannot flee.
J- oker . . . she has giggles and chuckles, on the way to laughing tracks, and crazy sense of humor, very funny jokes she cracks.
K- eeper . . . to her, one can depend on, secrets are only to her, she's someone worthy of trust, not a gossip, not a murmur.
L- istener, leader . . . a true born leader she is, a straightforward fearless host, and a powerful speaker, but a good listener at most.
M- other . . . not biologically, not a foster nor a step, she's a maternal Figure, a genuine and an adept.

N- urse, numerologist . . . a caregiver she is too, faultless nursing she has done, as good as her memory with numbers starting from one.
O- ptimist . . . she is one who never sulks, for she always finds a way even when things reach a cram, she always brightens her day.
P- oet, psychologist . . . the words that flow from her mouth, are as witty as her brain, with such love of making poems, there is something sure to gain.
Q- uestor . . . she is an adventurer, she exceeds her boundaries, she could separate the same and unite the contraries.
R- eader . . . the knowledge one gains from books, shows an image of her highness, broadening mentality, a clear woman of prowess.
S- inger . . . when words turn into music, when her speech turns into a song, a beautiful melody, one is ought to sing along.
T- urtle lover . . . she's very fond of turtles, and turtles are fond of her, amazing person she is, as fourteen turtles' mother.
U- ltimatum . . . a woman of principle, her first is always final, she sticks with her decision, no turns, no doubts, no denial.
V- irtuous . . . blameless in structure apart, pure in mind, body and soul, a woman of great virtue, her spirituality's whole.
W- riter . . . she does speak what she does write, she does write what she does speak, her mind's working both means, she is using it at its peak. She's extraordinary, her swift wits are really quick.
X - traordinaire . . . she is unpredictable, she is smart and she is slick, she's extraordinary, her swift wits are really quick.
Y- outh fullness . . . these are the cherish moments, she is very young at heart, she patterns herself with age, enjoying her social part.
Z- oolander . . . a lover f animals, carrying an unmatched care, a giver of hope and life, rescuer of unaware.

By Francis John Angelo Jimenez

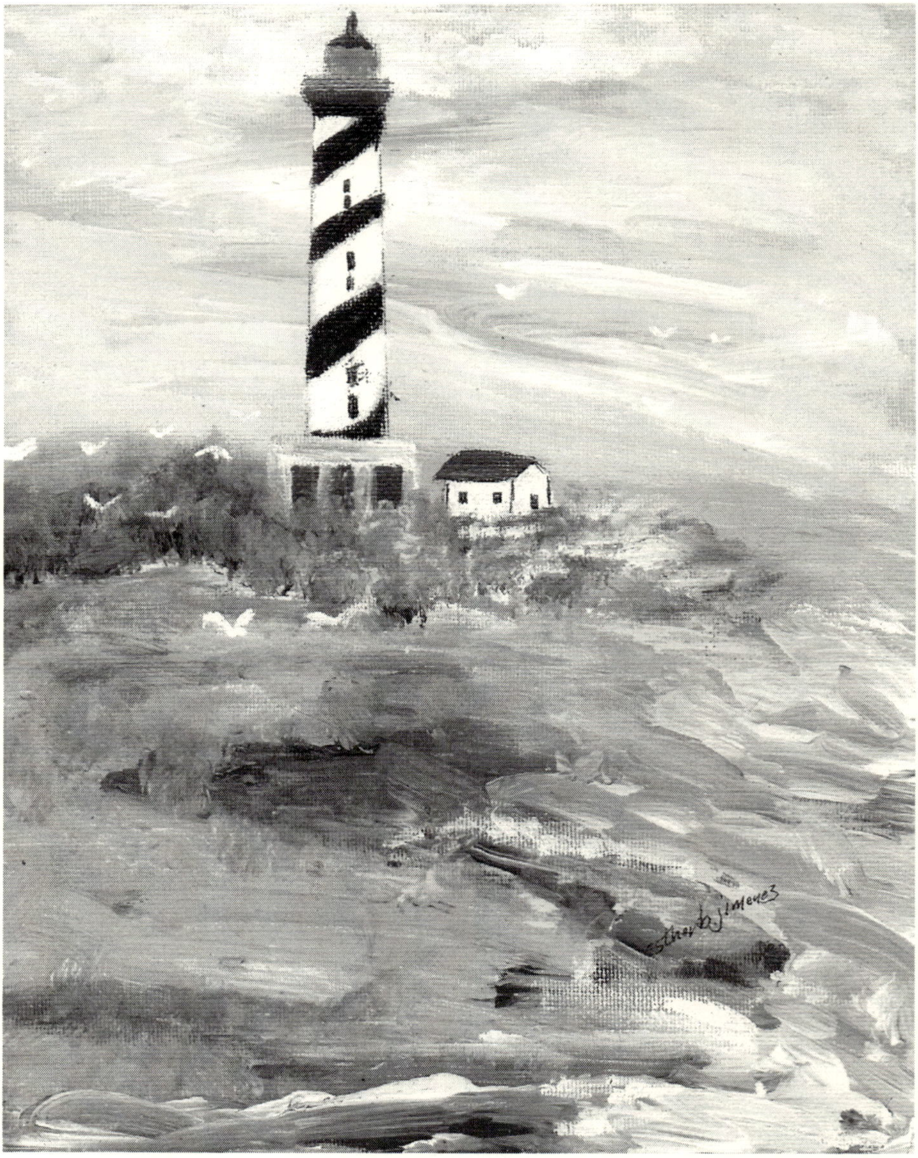
esther b. jimenez

DIVERSITY OF POEMS AND POETRY

I have written almost five hundred poems/poetry in a two volume set of books. I intended to split them into two sets, because I didn't want to make it to a very thick and heavy anthology. And I did, so I have two volumes of "What's In My Heart?" for you, my dear readers. I have extra poems/poetry in this category and about less than ten of them. It is too soon for the volume III, so I am including them in this book and I thought of entitling this chapter as," The Diversity of Poems and Poetry. The following poems didn't belong to any of the previous chapters nor any categories. Overall, my diversity of poems and poetry blends image language pattern meant to mark phases of my own process as well as to enlighten and inspire.

THE WALKING MARKET

Where can you see a place where the market
is served in front of you?
I have witnessed the simplicity of our culture
    . the simple life of the vendors
    . the delight I see in their faces
    . the routine walks they make
Yes, I love to be a Filipino by heart.

Early morning at dawn, I already am hearing
the word, "pandesal", a ten year old boy
selling freshly baked bread.
Thirty minutes later, another walking vendor
shouting, "taho," a semi-liquid soy bean
mixed with sugar syrup.

Then, more vendors heralding "isda"(fish),
alimasag (crabs), "gulay"(vegetables), "puto"
(rice cake).
Midday comes, there it is, a unique vendor
pushing a cart load of kitchen supplies, toys,
piggy-banks, children's clothes, knick-knacks,
brooms and more.

Then, between 3pm to 4pm I can hear another
vendor shouting, "binatog" (boiled kernels
of corn) with grated coconut and pinch of salt per order.
I also hear "banana-q" (sweetened native banana,)
"camote-q." (sweetened native potatoes).
These we called, "merienda" (snacks)

At dusk, there's the famous "balut" (duck prematurely
cooked, served with shell still hot, the vendor echoing
the word, "baluuutt", reaching the ears of the guys
drinking cerveza San Miguel, (the well known beer
in the Philippines.

Within the vicinity of our house, there are small "talipapa," (small fish, meat, vegetable market) and few "sari-sari" stores, (small stores selling candies, chocolates, biscuits, cookies, cigarettes, pops, school supplies and more.)

Not to forget, the visible "carinderia" or "turo-turo" restaurant, (a restaurant without chairs, but with long benches attached to the tables, and all you have to do is to point the food you want. Pointing means "turo," and that's where the "turo-turo" came from.

This is one thing that I enjoy every time I visit my loved ones and I love to re-feel and re-experience the Filipino ways of life. I feel good walking on the ground, feeling the January cool breeze early morning, listening to the birds' songs and the waking up calls by the roosters. Again, I enjoy seeing the daily walking market.

I know that you also have more memories to share from your time spent in our beloved land. One thing sure is, I am proud to be a Filipino. I feel the pride more, every time I am home.

THE AGONY OF WAITING

Be patient, as every inspirational book says
But the human limitation exists
How long can someone stand to wait?
A million dollar question, it is
Waiting is to stay in one place for something
or someone to arrive
to wonder, to ponder, to imagine how far
the mind goes
to be patient, to sacrifice, to linger with
the expectation
That certain someone would come in any
moment of time
The feeling of emptiness is a hard one
for the uncertainties occupy the whole space
it cracks your head, and drives you nuts
Alas! The enthusiasm, the excitement, the
interest are all gone
to wait no more, no more agony, no more
aggravation
I'm tired and bored of the word, "wait"
Enough for myself, enough for the time
Because my reply for this agony is to say
"Never mind."

SONGS' TITLES

These are the songs that we often sing in our community. They are all titles of the songs and I have at least twenty-two listed here.

Let Us Exalt His Name, together, forever;
The Blessing and Glory that, We Taste and See;
We Worship The LORD, we say, "I Exalt Thee"
More Precious Than Silver, that is, Our Father
Ascribe Greatness to our GOD Alone.
Salvation Belongs To Our GOD,
And GOD Is My Refuge
We Are Allowed To Enter In
Behold, Here I Am LORD
You Are My Delight, O LORD
The King Of Ages, We Will Magnify,
We Will Sing all the Psalms
Great And Wonderful You Are
To Love You and Make You Loved
Let Your Glory Fill Us and Our House
Let The Saints Be Joyful and Glory
Hallelujah! Hallelujah! Hallelujah!

This millennium thing scared a lot of people specially in the computer world. When we had our Weekend Power, I contributed something and I sang this song, based on the song, "High Noon,"

MILLENNIUM SONG

Do not forsake us, O Our Savior
On this our Judgment Day!
Do not forsake us, O Our Savior
Wait, wait along!

We do not know what fate awaits us
I only know I must repent
And we must face the man Who saves us
Or will we perish? Or will we be saved?
Now that we need Him by our side.

Ought to be born with love and mercy
Supposin' we lose the chance of eternity
Look at that big hand move along
Nearing Millennium!

He made a vow and said in Scriptures
Vowed to save us and be in His Kingdom
Be not afraid of death for oh . . . oh
And that's His promise!

Do not forsake us, O Our Savior
You made a promise as a vow
Do not forsake us, O our Savior
Although You're grievin'
'Coz we are sinning
Now that we need You in our lives
Wait for us, wait for us, wait for us . . .

PLAYBACK

Remembering, recollecting, recalling,
reminiscing, same meaning, same
thoughts and all was in the past.
You ponder, you dwell, on the
unforgettable, the memories.
You smile, you frown, you react,
Remember, it's all over.
In one incident, you focused and
shifted your thoughts
It was heart-breaking, you shook
your head
Another event, was heart-lifting
you nodded, you grinned
all these are very vivid, in one
corner of your brain
You learned from experience
experience is never a future
You can only benefit from your past
remember that!
Your past is your best teacher
As a student, be a good memory rewinder
Again, don't forget where we came from
because it is the bridge for your future
Live at present time and cherish
the moment of the past
You can only live once, not twice.

THE ALLEGORY OF THE HUMAN BODY

The Head of the family, is the Bread Winner
and the Backbone.
A Dirty Mind, needs a Brain washed.
The apple of ones eyes is the Adam's apple.
But the windows of the eyes,
cover the Pupils inside
The Stomach is upset, because of the butterflies
A Pigeon Breast is an anomaly
A Wishing Bone is the remedy.
Be careful of your brittle bones,
especially the Broken Hips.
You don't want to have a broken Heart
and to have a heavy chest
You don't want to be speechless and tongue-tied
So be anxiety free and not depressed
You're lucky you can still walk
despite of your knock-knee and bow-legged
Good thing, nothing is wrong with your
Feet and Achilles Heel
But you can still let your fingers do the
walking, in case of emergency
You are sensitive with Onion Skin
You have a warm heart and you care
The Body words, work as in Body language
From the top to the bottom and its usage
The Gift of Life is one of the wonders
The study of the Human Body
Are all GOD's creations in the beginning
of history.

CELEBRATION OF LIFE . . . HAIKU

It's a wonderful
Day today, I thank GOD I
Am alive again.

Life is too short, right?
And so make the most of it
Let's enjoy this gift

That's the gift of life
That our LORD Has given us
Let us be thankful

Be happy today
Be thankful that you're alive
Tell GOD that you're glad

We are blessed to know
That we are loved by our GOD
We're so grateful, LORD

Be cheerful and think
How lucky we are my friend
We can walk and talk.

We can see and hear
We can even eat and sleep
Most ill people can't.

Let's celebrate life
It's one of the miracles
And GOD's mighty deed.

HAPPY BIRTHDAY EVERYDAY!

WHAT'S IN MY HEART?
IS GOD'S UTMOST LOVE FOR US.

Edwards Brothers Malloy
Thorofare, NJ USA
January 21, 2014